BORN
TO
SERVE

The Trailblazing Life of Sam Sutton,
Valet to Three Presidents

Samuel Sutton Jr., CSCM, USN (Ret.)

ISBN 978-1-0980-7527-9 (paperback)
ISBN 978-1-0980-7528-6 (hardcover)
ISBN 978-1-0980-7529-3 (digital)

Christian Faith Publishing, Inc.
832 Park Avenue
Meadville, PA 16335
www.christianfaithpublishing.com

Printed in the United States of America

Samuel Sutton Jr., Petty Officer Third Class, Okinawa, Japan, 1980.

Contents

Teaching Barack to Salute

On the morning after his first inauguration, President Barack Obama walked into the private residence on the second floor of the White House, a cigarette in his hand.

"Sam, where's a good place to smoke?"

"Mr. President, I think the greenhouse would be best."

I ran back and got an ashtray. Then I followed him into the humid room on the White House roof, crammed with lush plants and brilliant flowers. A greenhouse had been there since the mid-nineteenth century, and I had heard that it provided a favorite escape for the Lincoln family during the Civil War.

The new president lit his cigarette.

"Where did you grow up, Sam?"

"Kinston, North Carolina, sir."

"How long have you been in the military?"

"Almost thirty years, Mr. President."

"I need your help with something," he said. "Can you show me the right way to salute when I'm walking to a helicopter or meeting with our military?"

The president had never served in the armed forces. Back in Navy boot camp in 1979, it had taken me a bit of practice to learn how to salute. It wasn't as easy as it looked. I had been corrected many times before I finally got it right.

"Mr. President," I said, "I'd be happy to help you."

He placed his cigarette in the ashtray, and we faced one another, standing at attention. I asked him to salute. I saw that his upper arm hung down a bit rather than being held at the horizontal. I went through the process with him, step by step.

"Sir, hold your hand like this, at about a forty-five-degree angle. When you position your hand, look at your palm from the side. That's right, Mr. President, just like that. Tip your hand a little bit more this way. Good. Now, when you bring your hand up, put a little snap into it. That's right—just like that."

For the next few minutes, I demonstrated, and he followed my lead. Now and then, I reached out to adjust the president's hand or the angle of his arm. Pretty soon, we were snapping salutes at each other like clockwork.

As a career military man, I had sworn to bear allegiance to the United States and to obey the orders of the president, no matter who that was or what party he or she belonged to. But Number 44 was something special. I had spent the last nine years serving as a valet to presidents Bill Clinton and G. W. Bush, but now I was serving the country's first black president. Having grown up poor in Kinston, North Carolina, I was proud of his election in a way that went beyond my usual pride in serving my country. I had come up the hard way, one of eleven children raised by a father who lived paycheck to paycheck as a long-haul truck driver for thirty-five years and a mother who cooked and cleaned and scrubbed for other families when she had more than enough exhausting work waiting back home.

As President Obama and I saluted one another, I was in awe of how far I'd come. The president didn't know that I had grown up in a house with no central heat and no hot water for baths or showers. That my family and I walked three and a half miles to church each Sunday and three and a half miles back because we didn't have a car. That I picked tobacco for nine hot southern summers, from age ten until I joined the Navy at nineteen (and finally took the first hot shower of my life).

But the president didn't have to know these things, nor did I have to know much about his life, in order for me to feel a special bond with him as a fellow black man.

When Obama was elected in November 2008, I had been thinking of retiring after twenty-nine years in the Navy. Then in December 2008, just before his inauguration, President Bush hosted a luncheon for the president-elect and all the living former presidents—Jimmy Carter, George H. W. Bush, and Bill Clinton. While I was ironing in the valet's office, President Bush's personal secretary called me into the Oval Office to meet Obama.

The president-elect walked up to me, his smile warm, hand extended in welcome. It was like meeting Dr. Martin Luther King.

"Sam, I've heard so much about you. I'd like you to come work for me."

In an instant, those retirement thoughts flew out the window. It was an opportunity I couldn't pass up.

"Yes sir, Mr. President."

Now I was teaching Barack Obama, my hero, how to salute.

I wondered what it would be like to have a black man leading our country. I had accompanied presidents Clinton and Bush on many motorcades, where entire city blocks were shut down for their arrivals. But I never saw them stop in a black neighborhood. When President Bush visited Graceland in June 2006 with Japanese Prime Minister Junichiro Koizumi, an Elvis fan, we had to drive through the hood to get there. Lots of little black and Latino kids were lined up along both sides of the street waving like crazy, yet Bush's motorcade just barreled through non-stop. When the presidents went through the rough neighborhoods, I hated to see little black kids standing there as the motorcade swept past. Why couldn't our presidents stop everywhere for everyone?

As Obama and I saluted one another, the thought came to me that Clinton and Bush probably wouldn't have stopped on the block where I grew up. But maybe, just maybe, the first black president would be different.

After a little more practice, his salutes were perfect—crisp, ramrod straight, done with a snap. He looked good, and I felt good.

"That's the way, Mr. President," I said. "You've got it exactly right."

He thanked me, then said, "If I'm reelected, I want you to stick with me for the whole eight years."

"Mr. President, I will be proud to stick with you to the end."

We shook hands on it.

"Sam, it's a deal. Now I'm off to work."

I escorted him to the elevator, which he took down to the first floor.

Samuel Sutton Sr. (right) with cap on, age
14, with his brother and friends.

CHAPTER ONE

Poor but Didn't Know It

We heard Dad coming home long before we saw him. The rumble of his eighteen-wheeler truck, like a creature too hungry to behave itself. The moment we heard it, we looked up from what we were doing. Then we ran from the family room, across the porch, down the front steps, and gathered on the sidewalk, jostling into each other with excitement. His giant truck made the wide turn into our block, downshifting, gears grinding, and now we were jumping up and down. He parked in the field across the street, and we took off running. We hadn't seen him in a week or ten days, but we also knew his truck was filled with leftover boxes of apple turnovers that he hauled up and down the east coast.

The door to the cab swung open. He sat there for a moment, too exhausted to move, wearing his baseball cap and company shirt, chewing the stub of an unlit cigar. Some of my siblings climbed up on either side of him while he gathered up his stuff.

"How you kids been doing?" He handed us a couple of boxes of turnovers, got down from the cab, and we trailed after him, the younger ones grabbing for his arms.

"Give the man some peace," Mom cried cheerfully as we crossed the porch. "Let the man watch some TV and unwind a bit before we eat."

"You kids been okay?" Dad asked, as we spilled into the house, and my siblings handed Mom the boxes of precious pies. "You been minding Mom?"

"Can we have fried apple pie tonight?" I asked.

"Junior, you sure can," Mom said, "but not until you eat!"

Dad always ate first when he got back from one of his trips, a steak with gravy and onions. Only after he was served did we kids get our food—beans and franks with homemade biscuits, our favorite meal. We never could get enough of Mom's biscuits.

Dad asked Mom, "Esther, how've they been?"

In his absence, she had been compiling her list. "Well, Sam, Tyrone didn't do the dishes, and Samantha refused to take out the trash. And both talked back some."

Dad wasn't in any rush. He took his time eating. We always used the same plate at dinner, from the main meal to dessert. With eleven kids, Mom didn't want to wash too many dishes. That night, we ate the fried apple turnovers with ice cream off the same plate that held the beans and franks. When the meal was over, Mom turned to Tyrone and Samantha.

"Go outside and pick a switch off the tree."

When they came back with flimsy branches with lots of leaves, we tried not to smile at one another.

Mom said, "You go right back out and get the stiff ones."

We listened to the smack of the switch and the howls of protest, thankful it wasn't our turn.

Justice having been done, we relaxed in the family room, Mom in her wing-backed chair, us kids sprawled on the floor. Dad sat in his chair, the one we never dared to sit in unless he wasn't around. Now he smoked his cigar, the only one in the family who used tobacco, his habit whenever he returned from the road. We had only three channels on our black and white TV but didn't lack for entertainment. We watched the movies together while Dad cracked his jokes. His biting wit always reminded me of Redd Foxx. Stories about accidents on the road. About crazy truckers he met along the way. About outlandish conversations overhead at truck stop lunch counters. He put himself completely into every story, dramatically playing the parts.

As night fell and the TV glowed on our faces, we fell into each other's shoulders on the couch. Even Tyrone and Samantha were happy. We were all back together again.

Mom and Dad were married in 1952 in his family's house. The preacher who "gave them away," as we say in the south, was my dad's uncle, Rev. C. L. Sutton. Both my parents came from large families—my father was one of ten kids, and my mother had thirteen brothers and sisters.

Dad was the main breadwinner; Mom was a teacher's aide for a couple of years and then cleaned and cooked for families. But even with two parents working, there were lots of kids and lots of bills to pay. There were eleven of us, born from 1950 to 1972—Larry (my half-brother), Patricia, Peggy, Wesley, Janice, Me (born June 9, 1960, right in the middle), Tyrone, Beachey, Dalton, Samantha, and Sabrina. Mom could stretch a dime like no one else, but sometimes toward the end of the month, we ate white bread with sugar or mayo until Dad got home with money from his latest trucking haul.

We didn't think we were poor at the time, although we certainly were, looking back. Maybe we'd get five dollars on our birthdays, but we never had a party because Dad lived paycheck to paycheck. When he passed away years later, we had to pay for his funeral because he had been borrowing against his burial fund to make ends meet. We didn't have a car growing up, so we either had to get rides to school and church or walk.

Or rather, should I say, we didn't have a *reliable* car. Dad owned a '65 Cadillac with big pointy fins that Mom had paid for. No one else could drive it, so it sat at the curb while he was away. Which was probably a good thing. Quite often, he sailed through stop signs when the brakes didn't work.

Sometimes we needed to borrow more than one ride from neighbors or friends since there were thirteen of us that had to get somewhere.

My sister Pat had asthma real bad. We always felt sorry for her; sometimes she had so much trouble breathing, we had to fan her. One night, when she was around fourteen, she was suffering so much that Dad had to borrow a car to drive her to the hospital, but it broke down on the way. In those days, you had to pay the ambulance to take you to the hospital, so Dad carried Pat in his arms for about a mile and a half to the emergency room.

We had a refrigerator but no ice maker. In the summer, we went to the convenience store behind Mr. Taylor's house for a twenty-five-cent bag of crushed ice, but we never made it home with the whole bag. Being kids, we took our time and half of it melted. There was usually just enough left for my dad's sweet iced tea.

Our two-story house on East Grainger had no central heat and no hot water the entire time I lived there. There was a single gas heater downstairs in the family room. It was a rough deal in the winter. Turning on the kitchen oven helped some.

We had a shower, but Dad couldn't afford a water heater. So we took bird baths—we'd put a pan of water on the heater to warm it and cleaned ourselves with a washcloth. Or we laid a wet rag on the heater in the morning so we could wash up before school. I didn't have my first hot shower until I joined the Navy at nineteen.

We didn't have AC either. Most of the white families, even the poorer ones, had both central heat and AC, but not us. My brother's house today still has one gas heater and no hot water.

All of us kids shared bedrooms, and I shared a bed with Tyrone. In the winter, we took turns getting in first to heat it up for the other one. My oldest brother, Wesley, was the only one with his own room.

And there were roaches all over the place. If you found one on your food, you'd pick it off and keep eating. When people came over to the house to visit, we'd sometimes see a roach crawling up the wall behind them. We kids tried not to laugh, hoping our guests wouldn't see it.

Our small house hadn't been an expensive one, but my parents got gouged on the 20 percent interest rate. One of my brothers is still paying off his house today. No car, no phone, no hot water, no central heat, and predatory interest rates—that's the way it was for most black folks back in Kinston, North Carolina.

Our neighborhoods were segregated. We lived in the black part of town and had to walk through the white section to get to the mall.

But coming up, I never experienced racism face-to-face from white people. They treated us well, and everyone knew our family. We generally got along, and I never got into any fights.

We didn't have a lot of friends and didn't need them. We weren't kids who ran the streets and got into trouble. We were a tight, church-going family.

And we didn't need a lot to keep us entertained. We used to sit on the front porch and play a game: the first car that drove by was my car, and the next one was my brother's, and so on down the line. If my car was a Cadillac and Dalton's was a battered pickup truck, we'd all goof on him.

Another game was cutting pictures out of the *Sears* magazine. I'd paste a living room set on white paper. "This is my house," I'd tell my siblings.

"Oh yeah?" my brother would say. "Well, take a look at my front porch."

Mom and Dad didn't like us cutting up their magazines. I always doodled on them, putting mustaches on people. It annoyed the heck out of my father.

"Junior, let me at least read the newspaper before you do that," he'd say. He couldn't read but was always trying to figure out what was happening in the world.

Although we didn't have much, we celebrated Christmas in style. Mom and Dad hid gifts in the closet; when I peeked inside, I hoped the cap gun or the sketch pad was mine. We had candy, oranges, and apples on Christmas Day, simple but treasured treats that you don't see anymore. Mom was up cooking until 3:00 or 4:00 a.m. the night before—candied yams, fried chicken, and a dozen sweet potato pies. And we always had barbecue. Either someone cooked a pig for us or we bought ten pounds of takeout from King's Barbecue in Kinston.

We were never invited by our relatives to holiday dinners. Although we were well-behaved, they didn't want all us kids around. They looked down on my mom, judging her as having too many children. Being treated that way by our own family still hangs over my head today.

Dad gave us twenty dollars or thirty dollars each at Christmas. That was a lot of money for a truck driver making a hundred dollars a week. He warned us that he would take it back if we fought or broke our new toys. Sure enough, by the end of Christmas Day, all the money was gone, along with our elaborate plans for spending it.

We didn't drink or smoke, we didn't run in the streets, and we didn't have wild parties. Dad kept our hair cut close.

Every Sunday, we walked three and a half miles to the First Baptist Church on Rouse Road and sat on the left side, the same row of seats I sit in whenever I'm back home. Reverend Rainer was a true southern preacher—you really got the message from him. He's ninety-seven now and still preaching. I believed in God even as a young child, prayed to him three or four times a day, trusting in him to meet my needs, not my wants.

That's what Mom and Dad had taught us. Whenever we wanted something, they asked us: "Do you need it? Because we won't get it for you unless you do."

All of us wanted a bicycle growing up, but Dad couldn't afford more than one. We had a hard time with that—eleven kids, one bike.

"Hey, you've been on that thing for twenty minutes! It's my turn!"

"Give it back, I ain't done!"

"If you want this," Dad said, "you need to take turns."

I carried that attitude into adulthood. If I wanted something but didn't really need it, I used my money for better things.

I was baptized at thirteen by Reverend Rainer, the last of my brothers and sisters to do so since I couldn't swim a lick and even an inch of water scared me. I was highly nervous when I got to the head of the line in the front of the church, wearing my white gown. Reverend Rainer dunked me in the big tub, and I survived. My son Sam got baptized at eleven in the same church.

Mom started cooking on Sunday mornings before we left for church, and when we got back, we ate good old southern food—fried chicken, mac and cheese, pig's feet, and pig's tail. And plenty of Mom's homemade biscuits with molasses. Sometimes I'd eat as many as six at a meal.

When Dad wasn't out on the road, his hobby was promoting gospel shows twice a month in Kinston, as well as in the nearby towns of Greenville, New Bern, and Goldsboro. He staged the weekend events at public schools, community colleges, and churches, featuring such well-known performers as Aretha Franklin, Shirley Caesar, Rev. James Cleveland, the Clark Sisters, the Staple Singers, the Blind Boys of Alabama, the Dixie Hummingbirds, and the list goes on and on. There were even two black ladies, Siamese twins joined at the head, who sang gospel. They scared me a bit when they walked out on stage, but once they started singing, I forgot all about it. Mom often invited the singers to the house for dinner.

I was six years old when I saw Aretha sing for the first time. When she became big, she didn't come down south as much. The male gospel singers always had female company at their hotels. Left lots of pregnant girls behind in every town they went to.

Since we didn't have a telephone, Dad had to walk over to the pay phone by the Kinston post office to arrange his shows. He'd make a short collect call to the singers and ask them to call him back.

Tickets were five dollars in advance or ten dollars at the door, but Dad didn't get rich. He'd have four or five groups singing for two or three hours, but sometimes there were only fifty people in the audience. Back in those days, gospel singers didn't care about the money—they were there to sing gospel. My father often paid them out of his own pocket, but it remained his hobby of love for twenty-five years, until he died of colon cancer at age fifty-five.

My sisters Pat and Peggy performed as The Supremes in talent shows back in the 1960s. It was two dollars to get in, and the crowd went wild when they came out lip-synching as Nancy Wilson and Florence Ballard (someone else always played Diana Ross). Me and my brothers lip-synched as gospel singers back home, using a broom as a guitar while a record played in the background. Dad got a real kick out of it.

If he made any money after one of his shows, he'd bring home fifty-cent barbecue sandwiches from King's Barbecue. Two big bags shining with grease. Good old North Carolina barbecue made with vinegar, not sauce. Every time I go back home and have a barbecue sandwich with hush puppies and coleslaw on the side, I think about my dad.

My maternal grandma, Annie Jones, lived out in the country about twenty miles from Kinston. When we visited on weekends, we all slept on the floor of her small two-bedroom house. Chickens ran in the yard, and birds sang loudly in the morning. I sang back to them as I lay on the floor, and when the birds finished whistling in return, I knew it was time to get up.

My grandma washed clothes for the white people who owned the land. Her rented house seemed almost like slave quarters. Two bedrooms, a living room, and a small kitchen, heated by a space heater. Surrounded by cornfields, which she walked through to get to the big old mansion where she worked. She still had an outhouse in the 1960s. How much I hated to use it in the middle of the night.

Whenever I crossed Grandma's porch, I often thought of my mom's sister Merle, who was killed by her boyfriend in 1968 when she was in her twenties. They were at a club, and the boyfriend stabbed Merle while they were in his car. He drove to my grandma's house and put Merle's body on the porch, where she died. She left behind two children who were raised by my mother's older sister, Aunt Rose. Mom was devastated; she had lost her baby sister. The boyfriend served ten years.

My father's father was C. L. Braxton, a white man from Greenville, North Carolina, a fact which I only learned after Dad's death. Then I understood why I had sisters and brothers who were lighter than I was.

My sister Samantha found this out only in 1997 when she was working at DuPont. A coworker heard her speaking about our father, and it turned out the coworker was Braxton's grandson. He asked his relatives about the story, and it turned out to be so. Braxton's grandson met my mom. Maybe someday we'll all get together to explore our common family history.

One of the only two photos I have of my dad is of him and his half-brothers playing baseball with his white father. I have no photos of me taken before the fourth or fifth grade and only three or four photos of myself as a child, at most.

My father was raised and later adopted by a black man named Wes Sutton. His mom was Rosebell King. Mom's dad, Erzel Jones, was part Native American, although I'm not sure what tribe (who knows—maybe my family has ties to a casino somewhere down south). He was a mean guy, Mom told us. Her mother was Annie Newkirk. Mom said she lost a lot of siblings who died in childbirth.

My parents always cared for people. Although they had a hard time making ends meet, Mom helped our neighbors furnish their homes. She bought furniture at yard sales and put it in storage in a shed out back. If she heard a neighbor needed something, she'd give it away. My sister told me she helped three families furnish their homes that way. Dad frequently gave away his last dollar, even if the person took that dollar to the liquor house. If the neighbor across the street, Ray Brown, needed two or three bucks, my father always had it for him, even if it was all he had left.

He was an easygoing man, unless you did something he thought was wrong.

One Friday night, when I was around ten years old, I stayed at my maternal grandma's apartment in the projects without telling him. She had moved there after living on the farm became too much to manage. When I got home on Saturday morning, he whipped my hide off with his belt buckle, the whippin' of my life.

But like he always did, he apologized after it was over.

"Junior, I'm sorry, real sorry, but you know it was for your own good."

I never used my belt or hands on my son because I don't believe in it, but that's how it was when I was coming up. Teachers and neighbors used to spank kids, and everyone was okay with it. Today kids talk back at you, and if you take a hand to them they'll call 911.

One Saturday morning, when I was ten years old, my aunt came by and asked Mom if her boys wanted to work in the tobacco fields. I volunteered to do it and did so for nine summers, from the age of ten until I joined the Navy. Ralph Jones, the white tobacco farmer, came to pick us up in town. A half dozen of us black boys rode in the back of his truck.

My job was to gather the leaves that the croppers had dropped when they picked the tobacco and throw them on the back of the trailer. I was making five dollars a day, twenty dollars a week, a lot of money back then. We started work at around 6:30 a.m. and knocked off around 4:00 p.m., so it came to about sixty cents an hour. Mr. Jones' kids—Donny, Troy, and Betty—also helped out in the fields.

We worked from June to August, and by mid-summer it was ninety degrees nearly every day.

That was how I made money for clothes and food. From that point on, nothing came out of my parents' pockets. I asked Mr. Jones to pay me at the end of the week instead of every day, to make sure I saved it. Then on Saturdays, I'd take my twenty dollars and buy clothes, shoes, and school supplies in downtown Kinston. With whatever I had left over, I bought myself candy that I kept hidden in my room from my brothers and sisters.

When I got a little older, I moved from picking up tobacco leaves to cropping. This paid a lot more—twenty dollars a day—but I didn't like the work because my hands got sticky from the leaves and I was afraid of snakes, which were plentiful in the fields. I also had a habit of taking too many leaves instead of only those that had changed to yellow green, just right for the picking.

"Junior," Mr. Jones would say from his tractor, "take only two or three leaves, not the whole stalk."

For some reason, I couldn't get it right, so they switched me to looping tobacco around a wooden stick, to be stored in the barn to cure.

Eventually, I moved on to working in the barn. Mr. Jones' son Troy would be in the loft, someone would be on the ground, and I'd be halfway between them on the ladder, passing the tobacco leaves up to Troy. It would take a week to cure about three hundred sticks of tobacco.

Betty Jones had a radio going in the fields, and it was a real treat listening to all the white singers I never heard. At around nine thirty, Troy would bring us a snack of peanut butter crackers. Mr. Jones was like a father to me, very good people. He was a white man, and we kids working for him were black, but he treated everyone fairly and with courtesy. We drank water from the same ladle, like one big family.

At lunchtime, Mr. Jones would drop us off at a store at the edge of the tobacco fields, where we bought chicken salad sandwiches, chips, cokes, and moon pies. Somehow the prices went up the moment us black kids walked in. Only if we protested would the white owner give our money back.

When I was twelve, Mr. Ralph taught me how to drive a tractor as I sat in his lap and he showed me how to shift the gears. One day, I fell off and broke a shoulder but went back to work wearing a cast because I wanted to make money. At fifteen, he taught me how to drive a pickup truck. I finally got my license in the twelfth grade after failing the test ten times (the instructor would fail you for looking at him the wrong way, and I froze up every time I saw him). When I was driving to Mr. Jones' farm one day, my brakes failed at a stoplight, but thank God there was a gas station on the other side of the intersection, and I rolled right in. God was watching over us.

It was hard work in the tobacco fields, but I was counting the money on Friday afternoon. By the time I went into the Navy at nineteen, I was making about $120, $150 a week.

I always had a job as a kid. During the school year, I cut grass and raked leaves for people and did other odd jobs. I always had a little job somewhere. My brothers and sisters worked in the summer, but I had one or two jobs all year round.

There was a black blind man living on Chestnut Street around the block from us. When I was around seven or eight years old, he'd stand on the sidewalk and call to us on the porch, "Can you ask Esther to have Junior take me to the store so I can cash my check?"

I would walk with him the two or three blocks. While he cashed his check, I watched the cashier carefully (she was the white owner's daughter) because she would hand him a dollar bill and say it was a five.

"No, ma'am," I'd say, "that's a one."

"Oh, so it is, my mistake."

She stopped after I caught her a second time. Then I did a little grocery shopping with him.

"Junior, can you get me some grits and some eggs? Thanks, young fella."

Mr. Taylor owned Kinston Wholesale down the street from us. He had asthma and paid me to help him on his boat, which he kept docked in Morehead City. I couldn't swim a lick but was game about helping out. When I untied the line, he took off from the pier with me sitting on the front end, scaring me half to death. Still, I loved the ocean. Sometimes we stayed out for six or eight hours at a time, and on occasion, he let me drive the boat. I went out fishing with Mr. Taylor every weekend in the summer, after working half a day on Saturdays in the tobacco fields.

In seventh grade, I had a crush on my white math teacher, Ms. Rice. Her husband owned a Chrysler dealership in Greenville, about thirty minutes from Kinston. She was the sweetest teacher I ever had, not a mean bone in her body. She helped each student in a personal way.

I always sat in the back of the class because I didn't want anyone calling on me. I was self-conscious about the way I spoke, rushing my words. I was a tall, skinny kid with pimples and thick eyeglasses, so much taller than the other kids that they assumed I had been left back. They called me "Sammy," which I hated. Terribly shy, I didn't like to talk to anyone and certainly not to girls. Even when I was working for presidents, I was very nervous when I had to set a glass of water on a podium in front of a packed stadium.

I could never get up in front of the class, but Ms. Rice took me under her wing. I became an A student and came out of my shell.

Back then, algebra was a class I stayed away from. I figured all I would need in life was basic math. My dad couldn't read, and I may have gotten my fear of school from him. But Ms. Rice helped me to learn math and not be afraid of it.

But I was still introverted and preferred hanging out in my room and doing my homework. I was always working a job and didn't have a car to drive around in. I played with my brothers in the park and street, but I was never any good at sports. Picked last, I often ended up on the losing team (or, shall I say, I didn't help the team win).

Ms. Murphy, my English teacher, used to date my dad back when he was a teenager (maybe that was the reason I passed). He married my mom at seventeen, so I guess Dad was a bit of a rolling stone. I found out only recently that he had a daughter with another woman, so I have a half-sister I never met somewhere in North Carolina.

I got interested in art in the ninth grade through a teacher named Mr. Cardelli, a short Italian guy. I did a lot of pencil drawing and sketching and always carried a pen in my pocket to write things down and do puzzles. I liked to draw buildings from photographs, like the Empire State Building. That's when I decided I wanted to be an architect. My high school named me Artist of the Year in 1979. There were five or six kids who I thought were a lot better than me, so it was a surprise. I still have the trophy and newspaper clipping.

We may have been poor without noticing it, but when I was a teenager, I began to realize just how short our end of the stick really was. I understood that Dad wore his trucker's uniform around the house because it was the only clothes he had. Everything we kids wore was handed down from our older siblings. Mom went to yard sales every weekend. I hated hearing her say, "Hey, Junior, try this shirt on." I'd go to school with holes in my pants or socks. Sometimes I stuck paper into the bottoms of my shoes so my feet wouldn't get wet in the rain. I never liked hand-me-downs, the same way I don't like leftover food. To this day, I eat it all at once, leaving nothing for the next time.

Kinston had two movie theaters downtown, one for blacks and one for whites. Although segregation was no longer legal, it was a fact of life. I'd go to the black theater with my siblings, and we'd watch the movie twice, hiding under the seats after the first audience emptied out.

Blacks and whites sat on different sides of Lovick's Café on Heritage Street, where we ate dough burgers—a deep-fried lump of dough with a little bit of beef inside. We drove past other restaurants that we knew were for white people only.

We lived on one side of the tracks, separated from the white people and the more well-to-do blacks. We'd see them and wish we were like them—the children of lawyers and teachers who wore nice clothes while we were barely getting by.

That's how the town of Kinston was set up. The baseball field was in a mixed neighborhood, but the elementary school was 99 percent black. There was only one white kid in the school. And there was only one black kid in the white elementary school, a kid name Kevin who I played with. His middle-class family lived in a white neighborhood.

Middle school and high school were more mixed. I had my first white friend, Randy, when I was in high school, but as close as we were, we never visited each other's homes.

That's when I realized how separated we were.

When I was a teenager, my mother started working for white families to bring in extra money, washing their clothes and cleaning their houses. It deeply pained me to see that. Not because of race, not because of a black and white thing, but because my mother was an older person doing all the toughest jobs for another family when her children needed her at home. But I kept those feelings bottled up inside.

To this day, I don't like having my son being taken care of by others. I vowed to spend every moment I could with him, and that's what I've tried to do.

I left the south when I was nineteen, but I've never lost my southern accent. Nor have I lost my southern ways. We talk to people. We help people out. People in New York walk past each other without saying a word, but in the south, we say hello to one another. Kids say "yes, ma'am" and "no, ma'am." We open doors. We thank each other. I've never lost those manners. I respect and care for everyone.

I recently took in an adopted teenager who lives around the corner. His parents had thrown him out, and my nephew Dylan saw him wearing the same clothes every day and sneaking in the school library or gym to sleep. Like a southern person would do, I let him live in my house, trusting him to cook and clean up after himself, and helped him get a job.

Growing up, we trusted each other. If you had my back, I had yours.

But when I go back south today, I feel a sense of sorrow. The houses are still rundown. Drugs and gangs have taken root. No one seems to care about "small-town America."

People keep their doors locked. Trust is gone. People fear one another, whether it's a white guy with tattoos or a black guy with baggy pants. A rough crowd now hangs out on the street where I grew up. There are bars on windows, which I never saw until I visited New York in the eleventh grade.

Gazing up at the high rises, I asked, "What are those things?"

"Bars, to keep people from breaking in."

"For real?"

I had never seen that down south, not when I was coming up. We left the doors and windows open at night. Neighbors came by to visit and to help us out. Back then, everyone watched out for other people's kids: "When your mama gets home, I'm gonna tell her what you've done."

I still miss those good old days.

When I graduated from high school, I had dreams of going to college and becoming an architect, but Mom and Dad were clear that it wasn't going to happen: "There are four kids ahead of you, and we don't have the money."

Luckily, I had a backup plan. My cousin June was a master chief in the Navy, stationed in Norfolk, Virginia. He used to talk to me about joining up when we'd sit on the front porch, how I could see the world and have career opportunities. He said I could learn to be a draftsman in the Navy, which was a lot closer to becoming an architect than working in the tobacco fields. I figured I'd join up for four years, get out, and then pursue my dream.

In 1979, I joined up under the delayed entry program, which meant I had a few months back home before shipping off to boot camp. I thought I'd work one more summer in the fields to pick up some extra money, but I didn't last two days. I could no longer stand the heat, the dirt, the backbreaking work of bending over for hours to pick the sticky leaves.

If I had any last doubts about leaving my old life behind, they disappeared for good under that relentless southern sun.

CHAPTER TWO

Seeing the World

In September 1979, Dad drove me to the recruiting station in Raleigh in his old Cadillac (lucky for us, his brakes worked). I stayed overnight and the next morning boarded the bus to Orlando, a twelve-hour ride. Two other recruits shared the cabin with me, headed for eight weeks of Navy boot camp.

There were no second thoughts until I got off the bus and the company commanders started screaming at me. "*You country boy! You idiot! Why you standing there looking stupid? Get off the bus! Give me two push-ups! Two push-ups now!*"

What the heck was that? The recruiters hadn't mentioned this part. Nor had June, my cousin, who had been in the Navy for thirty-something years. If he had told me anything about boot camp, it went in one ear and straight out the other.

They separated male and female recruits. They marched us to the exchange where we all got the same haircut. No choice at all; they just scalped us.

They marched us to the mess hall, where we had thirty minutes to eat. Then we began our day—marching, running, and classroom work.

Petty officers ran the show. They woke us up at three in the morning, they hollered at us as we ran, they inspected us every day as we stood at attention. Our beds had to made perfectly, and our uniforms had to be flawless. The petty officers chewed us out over the smallest mistakes, instilling fear into us. But it never upset me. All my life, I had been smiling on the inside whenever someone argued with me or got in my face. I just couldn't get angry with people.

There was a ship on base where we trained, and we spent time on the shooting range. Never shot a gun before. Don't think too many of us were hitting the targets—at least I wasn't.

Most of us had joined up because of patriotism, but other recruits had a choice: jail or the military, something I hadn't heard of back home. The rest just wanted to see the world.

I didn't get calls from home because we still didn't have a phone back in Kinston. I wrote letters once a week, but no one responded. Dad couldn't write—his signature was just a scrawl—and Mom was too busy cleaning people's houses while trying to raise her own kids. Unlike a lot of the other enlistees, I didn't have a girlfriend to write to. I had never had one because I was very shy and always worked after school. So my social life remained pretty limited—I never went out to a club until I was stationed on Okinawa.

Despite the relentless intensity, everyone got along. My one best friend in boot camp was Tony Castile, a white guy from Utah. He got boxes of goodies from his family while I didn't get anything. I had had white friends since high school, so it wasn't such a big adjustment, but I'd never met an Asian person before I joined the Navy. Meeting all different kinds of people made me more outgoing.

Tony could sing real well. There was a group of us who sang in church every Sunday. Mom had tried to get me to join the church choir back in Kinston, but it wasn't until the Navy that I wanted to join the base's choir for Baptist services. I auditioned for the company commander by singing "Amazing Grace," but I didn't make the cut.

To this day, I sing a gospel song quietly to myself every morning, thanking the Lord for the day, a southern thing. My mom did it, and I still do it. When I'm alone, I sing a little louder.

During boot camp, I was served food I had never seen before—asparagus, brussels sprouts. The vegetables we ate back home were butter beans, black-eyed peas, string beans, and collards. And believe it or not, it was my first time having coffee. My parents never drank it. One thing the Navy never runs out of is coffee.

And it was in boot camp, at age nineteen, that I finally had my first hot shower.

The most grueling part of training was the mile and half run we did every day. I never ran back in school—the only people who did were the athletes—and I wasn't in shape when I joined the Navy. We had fifteen minutes to run the mile and a half, and I barely made it. I wasn't the only one who had trouble.

The other grueling part was the swimming test. Like a lot of black people down south, I couldn't swim a lick. We had to jump off a diving board into a twelve-foot pool, remove our pants, inflate them by blowing air into them, and wrap them around our necks as a flotation device. All you had to do was float for two minutes. There were lifeguards all around to help anyone who had trouble, but I just couldn't do it.

I kept getting in the back of the line with two fellows from Alabama, Ralph and Bubba. I tried to hide behind them, although I was one of the tallest guys in Charlie Company.

I ended up failing boot camp because of the run and swimming tests. They gave me an extra two weeks to pass them. I felt like a flunky among a group of strangers—everyone had passed except me and one other guy. No one said anything, but I read mocking questions in their looks. *You can't swim? You can't pass a simple PT test?*

Thoroughly discouraged, I tried to get out of boot camp and go back home. I was fed up and thought the Navy just wasn't for me. I'd go back to Kinston and try something else. I begged my petty officers and the company commanders to let me out. I made up stories: Mom was sick back home and needed me.

The officers reached out to my mom to see if everything was okay. Then they took me aside: "Seaman Recruit Sutton, we'll work with you for the next two weeks to make sure you pass the swimming test. All you need to do is float."

When they supported me, when I truly understood they wanted me to do well, that was the turning point. I prayed every night, asked for God's help, and finally passed.

My sense of pride was immense—passing boot camp was one of the greatest accomplishments of my life. It took me ten instead of eight weeks, but I did it.

Graduation arrived, and at the ceremony, we marched in front of the officers, eyes right, carrying the flag. First time I saw an admiral.

Now I had high hopes that I would not only see the world, but that the Navy would give me a head start in becoming an architect.

After boot camp, I spent two weeks on leave with my family and then, in November 1979, reported to my first duty station aboard the USS *Sampson*, a guided missile destroyer, in Mayport, Florida.

I felt anxious, even a bit of fear, when I saw the ship anchored at the dock—a steel-gray behemoth, 170 feet in length. Now it was the real thing. I saluted the flag, asked permission to board, and climbed the gangplank, the sea bag heavy on my shoulder.

I served on that ship for the next eleven months, a radically new life, living on the ocean 24/7. Based on my test scores at the recruiting station, I automatically became a boatswain or bosun's mate, the traditional assignment for new recruits who didn't have a specific career path, such as cook or draftsman. My job was to paint, clean, and drive the ship. Shine the brass work. Swab the deck. Stand watch on the fore and afterdeck. Not to mention hanging over the side of the ship, gripping a rope held by a petty officer, while I painted the mammoth anchor (and I still couldn't swim a lick).

My favorite part was driving the *Sampson*, controlling a big wheel on the quarterdeck, listening to the duty officers on deck give their commands.

"Turn eleven degrees rudder."

"Aye, aye, sir, eleven degrees rudder."

A billion-dollar ship under my control. Hard to believe that I could give the wheel a spin and it went wherever I wanted it to go.

I recall driving the ship past icebergs in the Atlantic. Once in a while, I'd see a sub's periscope sticking up out of the waves.

Daily life on board was hectic. Reveille was at 6:00 a.m. A quick shower to conserve water, breakfast in the mess hall, and all hands on deck at 8:00 a.m., where we reported to our stations, received orders, and listened to briefings.

When I reported to the commander that all was well, I had to sign off with certain language that I could never remember. Couldn't read that good, and there were some tough words in there. I always got tongue-tied and dreaded that interaction because I knew I would mess up.

But Commander Chambers handled it well. Whenever I forgot something, he would fill in the blanks for me.

"I want you to learn this," he said, "because it's an important sign off." It was only half a paragraph, but I had such a hard time memorizing it.

We stood watch for four hours at a time. When we drilled for military action at sea and fired our guns, the heat and smoke burned the paint off the ship. We sanded the sides and painted them haze gray again. By the time we sailed back to port, standing topside in our full uniforms, the *Sampson* was perfect.

We met up with cargo ships to refuel at sea. If something went wrong, we had to cut the lines. The ships were only about a hundred feet apart.

Living on board meant real tight quarters. As an E-1, a bosun's mate, I had to sleep on the top bunk. But we all got along, and everyone worked as a team. There was no conflict, racial or otherwise.

Oddly, I never got seasick crossing the stormy Atlantic, but I became sick as a dog in the calm Caribbean. After I made it through that, I knew I could be a sailor.

And I saw much of the world, mostly Europe and the Caribbean. London was the first foreign city I ever visited. In the Caribbean, we went ashore for dinners, but unlike most sailors, I never drank and chased women when we were in port. Probably 80 percent of my crew went to prostitutes, but I wasn't brought up that way. Those girls could have been my sisters. Later in my career, when I sailed to Thailand, I saw that the prostitutes were mere teenagers. Lots of guys came back drunk and had to get VD tests.

Instead, I preferred to stay on the ship while my shipmates were carousing. Only a small crew of us was left behind. Guys would pay us to stand watch for them while they went out and had a good time.

The lower ranks didn't have much money, and that was how we made it. If I loaned someone twenty dollars, I expected forty dollars back, and they paid it because they wanted to have a good time.

After serving as a bosun's mate for four months on the *Sampson*, a petty officer said to me, "Seaman Sutton, why don't you become a chef?" The draftsman position, which was my original choice, was filled up.

A lot of Filipinos had traditionally served as cooks in the Navy, dating back to the early 1900s when their country was an American colony, but they were looking for new people to enter the field. I wasn't much of a cook but got talked into it. It didn't come naturally, but what made it easier was that a lot of the food was precooked—just took it out of the freezer and microwaved it.

And I enjoyed working in the galley. Didn't have to paint the ship's anchor no more. Didn't have to stand watch at three or four in the morning. Had to make sandwiches at midnight for guys on that shift, but I didn't have to be on duty round the clock.

The hardest part was cooking while crossing the Atlantic. The seas were so rough that sailors didn't want me to cook fried food because the grease made them sick. Sometimes there were only a dozen people at meals, and they had to be tied to the mess tables because chairs were sliding every which way. I couldn't help dropping food and spilling soup. But I didn't get seasick.

I was serving breakfast on the *Sampson* one day. When I was in the galley getting some meals, an officer stuck his head in the door and said, "These eggs weren't cooked right, sailor. I'm sending them back. Next time, cook my eggs the right way!"

He embarrassed me right in front of the other sailors. I had never been spoken to so rudely.

"Yes, sir. Yes, sir."

I grabbed a fistful of scrambled eggs, smashed them down on his plate, and brought them out to the officer. I had a little bit of an attitude back then. I was new to taking orders and didn't like the way he spoke to me. I was surprised that I did that and never did it again.

Enlisted men did things like that because certain officers were real rude, especially those straight out of the Naval Academy. They had big egos and could turn on you and bring you down in a heartbeat. Some of the cooks routinely sabotaged their meals by dropping their food on the floor and pulling other tricks. What these new officers didn't realize was that the chief petty officers really ran the ship; if the officers got on their bad sides, the CPOs could make them look really bad.

When the *Sampson* came back to port all cleaned up, that was always a wonderful moment for me. I felt proud of my ship, proud of my shipmates, and proud of my country. Families were lined up at the pier waiting for us. Cars stopped on the bridge entering Mayport to take photos. We were lined up at attention in our dress whites and the flag snapped overhead.

White was my favorite Navy uniform, and I still have mine. I can't fit into it for the life of me, but I've saved it all these years.

I did well enough cooking in the galley that my superiors wanted me to be trained as a chef. So I left the *Sampson* after eleven months to attend mess specialist school (also known as A-school) in San Diego. There I learned basic cooking and baking skills.

After my training was completed, I was ordered to Okinawa, Japan. When I got the news, I had never heard of the place. Two days later, I flew out of San Diego on a 747, only my first time on a plane. Near the end of a fifteen-hour flight, I saw snowcapped Mount Fuji for the first time.

I reported to the commander of Amphibious Force One on White Beach on Okinawa, Rear Admiral George Shick, a two-star admiral and an old Navy guy. I became the admiral's driver. I picked him up every morning at six thirty and brought him home at four p.m. I wasn't doing any cooking—the galley was staffed with Japanese chefs—but I made him coffee.

I was stationed in Okinawa for two and a half years, from 1981 to 1983. We lived right on the beach. It was a small command, and I had a single room in the barracks. Years later, when I served as valet to President Clinton, I went back to White Beach to visit and tried to find Aki, a Japanese chef I had befriended. When I walked out of the NCO club, I saw him, and we recognized each other immediately.

"Hey, Sam! How're you doing?"

Aki might've been fifty years old but, like a lot of Japanese, looked years younger.

Okinawa was the first time I experienced an earthquake. The walls started shaking, and it was very scary.

Other than that, it was a dream assignment. When we got off work, we could play basketball or relax on what was our private beach. Our command played baseball games against Japanese military teams. At low tide, you could walk out to a big rock and sit on it, soaking up the sun. When evening came, I'd sit on that rock and breathe in the darkness. One time, we lost track of the tide, and the other guys swam back, but I had to wade. The water was up to my neck, but I made it.

I worked with a petty officer named Steve Shott, who is still my best friend to this day. Steve had already been stationed on Okinawa when I reported there, and he was a great chef. He showed me around the island with his girlfriend, Oh. There was a restaurant right outside the base, and that was the first time I had Japanese food. Every time I went there, they knew what I wanted—pepper steak.

There was a main downtown on Okinawa where I did shopping and sightseeing, but I didn't have much time for that because I had my duties driving the admiral, attending ceremonies at various bases, and helping the admiral and his wife host luncheons and dinners. I would do all the cooking and serve drinks.

We went out to sea for up to three months at a time on the USS *Blue Ridge*, the flagship of the Sixth Fleet, a six hundred-foot amphibious command ship with a crew of 1,200. My job was to attend to Admiral Shick. We also served Marine officers stationed aboard.

My routine was to wake up at 6:30 a.m., check the weather report for the admiral, and prepare his uniform for that day. I made his bed and did his laundry. Then I helped in the kitchen, but I didn't do a lot of cooking. I assisted the chef and served the officers at their meals. I'd also serve Admiral Shick in his small stateroom.

On the *Blue Ridge*, we'd sail to Japan, Thailand, and the Philippines, where we docked at Subic Bay. I walked around the town a couple of times, but it was mostly slums and very dirty, with a lot of young kids begging for money or swimming in the trash-filled water. There were prostitutes all around, and a lot of the guys came down with venereal diseases. As bad as the south could be, I had never seen poverty at that level.

Admiral Shick's wife always bought me presents for Christmas and my birthday, and the admiral gave me a book about Dr. Martin Luther King. They were good people and were easy to have a conversation with.

While stationed in Okinawa, I was awarded Sailor of the Quarter and then Sailor of the Year, based on my leadership and performance. There were over two thousand service members stationed in Okinawa, so it was quite an honor.

Pretty soon, my four-year enlistment was nearing its end. The Navy wanted experienced people to reenlist, and I did so when they offered me a five-thousand-dollar bonus to sign up for another six years.

Five thousand was a helluva lot of money back then.

Heck, still is today.

At Adm. Moreau's villa in Naples, Italy, 1986.

CHAPTER THREE

Moving Up the Ranks

In 1983, Admiral Shick left Okinawa to serve in the intelligence command in Alexandria, Virginia, down the street from the Pentagon. Many months before, he had told me, "Petty Officer Sutton, I'm going to help you get to DC someday."

I had given the admiral 120 percent, and now he was looking out for me. He reached out and put in a word for me to work for the Joint Chiefs of Staff in Washington. That was a tough position to get, and I was handpicked for it. That's what happened to me throughout my military career—I rose in the ranks and in responsibilities when officers saw the work that I did and my potential to advance. I never once asked for a position or lobbied for a promotion.

Along with my buddy Steve Shott, I was assigned to work in the mess of the chairman of the Joint Chiefs of Staff (JCS), where I served for the next three years. General Joe Vessey was chairman of the JCS at the time, making him the most senior officer in the US military, the president's principal military advisor. Lieutenant Holland was in charge of the mess, which fed the Joint Chiefs and their deputies, along with civilian and junior staff.

I really enjoyed being back in the states. I was in the kitchen a little bit, but they kept me mostly in the dining room, and that's where I got to meet everyone.

When General Vessey was hosting weekday dinners at his house, he always asked for volunteers to work for him. I was still on the mess staff for the JCS, but helping out at the general's house enabled me to earn fifteen dollars an hour in a side job. My hand went up every time General Vessey asked for volunteers. I really enjoyed going over to his home to serve dinners.

General Vessey's chef, Sergeant Major Stewart, must have been two hundred pounds overweight. You never saw him cook until the last minute, when everything miraculously came together. They had been trying to kick him out of the military for the longest time because he couldn't pass his biannual physical training test, but Vessey said that Stewart wouldn't retire until he retired.

Officers would arrive at the JCS mess as early as five a.m. My job was to set out fresh coffee, cream, and sugar before the chairman's personal staff arrived.

I was now serving the highest ranking officers in the military, but I wasn't at all intimidated. I had been accustomed to being around top brass since I worked for Admiral Shick. In addition, I had known many of the generals and admirals when they were junior officers.

I had always been a disciplined and organized person since I was a kid. It came naturally to me at a young age. When I raked leaves for people back in Kinston, I didn't want to leave a leaf on the ground. I remembered telling my brother, "Tyrone, get the rest of those leaves. Don't leave any behind." To me, raking leaves and leaving behind a nice looking yard was an art. It was the same way with my childhood bedroom. I kept it neat. When I picked up tobacco leaves at age ten, I made sure to pick up every last one. When I hung over the side of the ship and painted the anchor, I wanted it to look perfect.

No matter what I did, whether the task was big or small, I always did my best.

While I had served officers before, the admirals and generals I worked for in DC had even greater power. I was new to that. I tried to learn from them and emulate them—the way they carried themselves, how they were always professional, courteous, and very well-spoken.

I especially admired General Vessey. He had come up through the enlisted ranks to become a four-star general. He had joined the Minnesota National Guard at sixteen in 1939, lying about his age, and served in combat in the North African and Italian campaigns in World War II, as well as in Vietnam.

One of the sergeants who worked for Vessey in his home as part of his service staff was getting ready to move on. One Monday morning, I met with the general's chief of staff. He was a street-type guy, real professional but very funny.

"Sam, General Vessey would like you to come work at the house."

That Thursday, I reported for duty, the first enlisted man from another branch of service to work for the chairman of the JCS. If the chairman was from the Army, as Vessey was, the tradition was to have a service member from the Army serve him, but they saw me as the outstanding candidate for the job.

Mrs. Vessey was a sweet woman. Their son, a retired warrant officer, stayed with them. Once in a while, my job was to give him a ride to the State Department in the general's car. As part of the general's service staff, I cut the grass, cleaned the house, washed clothes and cars. Sergeant Major Brown, a fellow southerner like me who had been in the service for more than thirty years, showed me how to care for the general's uniform, since an Army uniform was totally new to me. General Vessey had a least thirty ribbons and stars that had to be put back in the same exact way after his uniform was cleaned, and it probably took me forty minutes to do it. I had to follow a diagram to get it right.

Mrs. Vessey loved her flower beds that were filled with white, red, and yellow roses, and she showed me how to properly cut them.

"Sam, when you cut a rose, you go down three leaves and then snap them."

The Vesseys' house was located at Fort Myer, overlooking Arlington Cemetery and the Washington Monument. The horse that pulled the caisson with JFK's body was buried there. The various Joint Chiefs lived in the same row of houses. I lived in the barracks at Fort Myer for a year until I found my own place.

Meals were served French-style at General Vessey's home, from platters to individual plates. I'd be holding a big platter that weighed at least ten pounds, hoping the guests would make their choices before the sweat dropped off the tip of my nose and into the food.

I served the highest ranking members of President Reagan's cabinet, such as Defense Secretary Caspar Weinberger, and General Vessey's military counterparts from Japan and Europe.

The Joint Chiefs met once a day in a secure, top-secret location called the Tank that required the highest clearance to enter. I would go in before they arrived and set up the coffee, water, and name tags. When I served people during meetings, they would stop talking as soon as I walked in and wouldn't resume until I left. Along one wall was a big screen TV used for briefings.

The Tank is where I first met President Reagan and Vice President Bush. Reagan was a tall, broad guy, a movie star wearing tailor-made suits who liked to banter with the Joint Chiefs. I never spoke to him, but Vice President Bush, who liked his coffee served with warm skim milk, once asked me my name.

"Petty Officer Sam Sutton."

"Nice to meet you. You in the Navy or Coast Guard?"

The first time I shook the hand of a future president.

Lots of enlisted people didn't work in the Tank. Only those who had the cleanest, most professional presentation, and the shiniest shoes were chosen for that assignment.

To this day, I never leave the house without shining my shoes.

When General Vessey retired in September 1985, he was replaced by Admiral William Crowe, who asked me if I wanted to stay on with him. At the same time, Admiral Arthur Moreau, a three-star admiral who had been a deputy to General Vessey, asked me if I wanted to come with him to Naples, Italy, where he would serve as commander-in-chief, Allied Forces Southern Europe. I chose to accept the assignment with Admiral Moreau.

General Vessey had a huge retirement ceremony at the Fort Myer, attended by President Reagan, Defense Secretary Caspar Weinberger, the Joint Chiefs, and military guards from all branches of service.

Two weeks later, I flew out to Naples with Admiral Moreau, his wife, Katie, and two of their five kids.

The admiral was the second naval flag officer I served after Admiral Shick. He always had a smile on his face, drank four or five cups of coffee a day, and smoked like a dragon.

The family lived in a ten thousand-foot villa with marble floors perched on the side of Mount Vesuvius, from which we had a spectacular view of the Bay of Naples. Two Filipino chefs who had been there about twenty years worked alongside me. Admiral and Mrs. Moreau asked me to live downstairs in the villa.

I had multiple tasks. There was a lot of that house to clean, and because of local air pollution, I was constantly cleaning it. Admiral Moreau's daughter Jo was seventeen and in the eleventh grade. She was always late for school, so the admiral asked me to drive her in the morning. She knew how to drive a stick, which I wasn't very good at, so as soon as we left the villa and turned the corner, we swapped seats in the small convertible. When the admiral found out, he asked me to do all the driving.

It was a military family. The admiral's two oldest sons were in the service (one was tragically killed in a flying accident) and their daughter Katherine was married to a two-star general.

Admiral Moreau hosted guests at the villa, such as General Colin Powell, who was stationed in Germany at the time, and frequently entertained with dinners and holiday receptions.

We did a lot of traveling, at least three weeks out of each month, to NATO headquarters in London and other countries in Europe, like Greece, Germany, and Turkey. Admiral Moreau had a yacht, and every weekend, we sailed to the island of Capri, a magical place, where we stayed overnight. They treated me like family.

The admiral was having heart problems because of his smoking. He went through at least two or three packs a day. As a precaution, Mrs. Moreau and some of the staff, including me, took CPR classes.

The admiral had had a slight heart attack some months before. After he came out of the hospital, everyone was begging him to quit.

When Italian military officers saw him pick up a cigarette, they tried to snatch it away from him.

At three o'clock in the morning, in December 1986, I heard a knock on my door and Mrs. Moreau's frantic voice.

"Sam! Sam, come upstairs!"

I dressed quickly and ran up the stairs. Admiral Moreau was stretched out on his bed. I had taken the CPR class a week or two before and knew exactly what to do. For the next twenty minutes I blew into his mouth and pressed down hard on his chest, sweating like a racehorse, as Mrs. Moreau prayed and cried.

"Oh God, please don't let him die."

"He's going to be okay," I told her, and said the same thing to myself as I worked on the admiral.

At times he seemed to be coming through. I was praying to God the whole time. *This can't be happening. Please God, don't let him pass away.*

An ambulance was on the way but couldn't find the villa, which was hidden behind a high wall. It finally arrived after forty minutes.

I got in the front seat with the driver. They kept doing CPR as they rushed him to the hospital. About two hours later, they pronounced him dead, but I think he died in the house. Mrs. Moreau and I broke down crying in the hospital room.

They flew his body back to Washington for funeral services at the Naval Academy.

Mrs. Moreau had me carry the American flag during the ceremony. At one point, we had to kneel during the Catholic service, which was foreign to me because I'm a Southern Baptist, but I followed everyone's lead.

It was the first time I heard taps against the backdrop of a silent cemetery, and it brought tears to my eyes. Haunting.

Several months later, I received the Navy Achievement Medal for trying to save the admiral's life, but I didn't consider myself a hero.

Had the ambulance arrived earlier, Admiral Moreau might have survived. One of the worst things I ever experienced. He had died at just fifty-five, the same age as my father.

I found out my father was sick when I was stationed in Naples in 1985. He didn't have much time left, so I was granted leave and went back to Kinston for a week and a half. I saw him in the hospital, then went back home. It was very hard for me to visit. I wanted to remember my dad as he was. The next day, friends drove from the hospital in Greenville to tell us he had died. My brother Tyrone was there with him, but because we still didn't have a phone, he couldn't call us with the news.

I had never seen Dad ill. He never went to the hospital. If anything pained him, he kept it to himself. But when he got laid off as a truck driver, he couldn't find work. They said he was too old to get hired. Sitting around the house, his health went down. Whenever I went back home to visit, he asked to borrow money, something he had never done before.

I extended my leave for three or four days so I could attend his funeral. About five hundred people came—family, friends, gospel singers, fellow truckers. My dad was a well-known man in Kinston and up and down North Carolina. The church choir sang, and we played songs from his favorite groups—Shirley Caesar, the Blind Boys from Alabama. The preacher gave a rousing eulogy.

I was a pallbearer with my brothers. When we arrived at the cemetery, my brothers and I misunderstood the funeral director and stood facing in the wrong direction to lift the coffin from the hearse. We had to turn all the way around, laughing at our mistake.

I had the feeling that Dad was laughing along with us.

After Admiral Moreau's death, General Robert Herres, who headed the Air Force's Space Command, asked me, "Sam, what are you going to do now? Going back to Italy?"

"No, sir, I want to make it back to DC." I was serving flag officers and felt I had more of a chance of continuing in that assignment if I was back in Washington.

General Herres had been picked as the first vice chairman of the Joint Chiefs of Staff in February 1987. His colonel called to ask me to serve with him in DC, so once again I returned to the states.

It took me three days to pack up all the household goods in Naples. Then Mrs. Moreau, Jo, and I flew back. I stayed in the barracks at Fort Myer and helped Mrs. Moreau get organized in her home for the next week until General Herres came to town.

During that time, Mrs. Moreau held a reception at her home, and I was serving hors d'oeuvres. I kept offering the tray to Admiral Carlisle Trost, the chief of naval operations. After I made two or three rounds past him, he finally said to me, "Sam, if you want to make chief petty officer, you can get this stuff out of my face because I'm getting tired of it." He was a real friendly guy and wasn't being serious, but I took the tray away real quick because as CNO he called all the shots. I made chief petty officer that same year.

Working for General Herres was a great opportunity. I had been handpicked for the position, and as with every position I had, I put my all into it.

I laid out his uniform in the morning. As his backup driver, I drove him to the Pentagon and returned home to attend to household duties. I cut the grass, washed the cars, and walked the dogs. Today, civilians perform those tasks, but back then, military personnel did it. I also served as the general's head chef.

I did a lot of traveling with General Herres. On a trip to Australia, I met Adrian Scott, the butler to the US ambassador to that country. We've been best friends ever since. He took me sightseeing in Australia, and I met his parents. When he served dinner at his house, I was expecting an Australian meal, since sampling local foods was one of the perks of my job, but Adrian served spaghetti. I still kid him about that.

I was close with Juanita, an enlisted aide who also served General Herres. When the general was away one time, I played a joke on her. I turned over a few chairs in the kitchen and lay down on the floor, pretending someone had broken in and knocked me cold. When Juanita saw me, she ran out of the house screaming.

There were MPs all around, but luckily none of them heard her.

Working for the general was a fun job, as it had been with admirals Shick and Moreau. We were a team and felt as close as family.

Cooking for the Joint Chiefs, 1985.

With Adm. and Mrs. J.P. Reason at reenlistment ceremony for my
brother-in-law Master Chief Larry Bowden, my sister Peggy on my right.

With Gen. Colin Powell, Chairman of the Joint Chiefs of Staff.

Receiving the Joint Service Commendation Medal from
Gen. John Vessey, Chairman of the Joint Chief of Staff.

CHAPTER FOUR ———————

Meeting My "Navy Dad"

The world of the high ranking officers was much more of a white one than the world of the ships and the lower ranks. In fact, almost entirely white. In boot camp and at sea, we were pretty mixed racially, worked as equals, and closely supported one another.

The upper ranks were another story. Now, working for admirals and generals, I wondered why I saw so few higher ranking black officers. It was a big deal if you saw a black captain in those days, let alone a full bird colonel with an eagle on his or her shirt. And there were far more Filipino and black sailors serving as enlisted aides; it was rare to see a white sailor in those positions. I felt it was very important for a black enlisted person to see a black officer who had made it up the ranks, but it wasn't something I often saw.

On a trip with General Herres to Seattle, I was carrying the general's bags to his room at the military base when I spotted Admiral J. Paul Reason. I knew he was the only black admiral in the Navy. At the time, he was serving as commander of the naval base in Seattle, where he was responsible for all naval activities in the states of Washington, Oregon, and Alaska. Previously, he had served as military aide to President Jimmy Carter.

I looked up at him and said, "Good morning, Admiral."

"Good morning, petty officer."

That was the extent of our conversation, but something told me I was going to work for him one day.

When General Herres retired in 1990, Admiral David Jeremiah asked me to stay on with him. Jeremiah was the second vice chairman of the Joint Chiefs of Staff. At the time, General Colin Powell was chairman of the Joint Chiefs, the first and to this date only black chairman of the JCS.

When Admiral Jeremiah retired a few years later, I worked on General Powell's staff while I was waiting for orders. I had known the general and his wife since my time in Naples when I worked for Admiral Moreau.

Powell was a quiet, thoughtful person. He didn't say that much. He struck me as proud and private. He and Mrs. Powell were polar opposites. She was completely down to earth, someone you could gab with like she was your mom, but the general wasn't one to sit around and chat. He was completely professional and always focused on the task at hand. Everyone looked up to him.

I had the sense that because he was a black officer, and a very high ranking one at that, he had to be a little more reserved, somewhat more careful about what he said or did. I knew that a black person had to do more than a white person, at whatever rank, to prove him or herself. You had to do double the amount of work and go that extra mile to prove you could do the job. When I worked for Admiral Jeremiah, I was the junior person on a staff of three. I was the chef and had to prove I was one of the best chefs in the military to show that I didn't need someone to watch over me.

I knew all this from experience. I knew it from seeing how hard my father and mother worked. I always remembered what my dad told me whenever he got back from one of his long-haul routes: "Junior, make something of yourself. Don't let them tell you that you can't do it."

We both knew what "them" meant. We had no ill will toward anyone, but we were men of the south.

While I was serving in Washington, I began volunteering to feed homeless people in the city. Mrs. Powell and Mrs. Jeremiah, who had already been volunteering, got me interested. I joined people from church groups and the Boy and Girl Scouts. We drove in a van three or four times a week, stopping at various sites to distribute soup and sandwiches donated by gourmet restaurants. I was stunned by the sight of hungry kids on street corners, shoving and pushing one another to get to the food. They were so aggressive that I told the volunteers to stay in the van. I did the work for two years and never forgot the desperation and poverty.

One day, there was a kid out there holding up his pants.

"Do you have a belt?"

"Never had one."

I took off mine and gave it to him.

"This is going to be too big," I told him, "but we can tie it with a knot."

When you got away from the Capitol and the White House, you saw the real Washington, the "chocolate city," as Admiral Reason later described it to me. We didn't drive with our donated food down Ambassador's Row. We didn't drive to the Naval Observatory or to the Jefferson Memorial. We drove to the black and Hispanic neighborhoods that were "the other side" of official Washington.

It brought back memories of my upbringing, when my parents were trying to raise eleven kids and the food was going quick. My mom had to ration what we ate (although we didn't ration her biscuits because they were so easy to make). As I handed out food to hungry kids, I remembered what we sometimes ate for dessert back in Kinston—a lot of sugar mixed with a little water and spread over white bread. One reason why I'm a diabetic today.

Mom would get a big block of welfare cheese, which, surprisingly, was the best cheese to eat with scrambled eggs and to make grilled cheese sandwiches

I don't think the government is doing enough to address poverty. Yet despite all the programs, the homeless still end up on the street. They don't like shelters, but aren't there any family members to take them in?

The same thing in Los Angeles. In downtown LA, I saw a mile of homeless people—older people, kids, drug addicts, you name it. I had never seen anything like that in the US. The only thing that came close was the poverty I saw in the Philippines.

People need to take responsibility, and families need to reach out. If my brother's sleeping on the street, I should help him and take him in.

That's what I did with Melvin, the son of a military friend who worked at Fort Myer. His parents were moving back to Puerto Rico when Melvin was fourteen or fifteen. They wanted him to finish high school in DC, but he had dropped out, so I let him move in. He lived with me for four years. I helped raise him, and he eventually went back to high school.

That's how we should take care of one another.

When General Powell retired, I worked for General John Shalikashvili when he became chairman of the Joint Chiefs in 1993. During that time, a new chance came my way.

A member of the Navy personnel department, who was looking out for people ready to fill new positions and get promotions, called me.

"Hey, Sam, a three-star admiral is looking for someone to come work for him. Do you want me to put your name in the hat?"

"Yeah, do that."

When I saw the admiral's photo, I recognized J. Paul Reason, whom I had met briefly out in Seattle. When he came to Washington with his wife to pick up his third star, I had an interview with him.

It was my first formal interview in the military. For all my positions in the past, I was recommended by word of mouth because all the officers knew each other. When one enlisted aide retired, they were on the lookout for a replacement. But with Admiral Reason, it was a sit-down interview with him and his wife.

I was real nervous. I had never wanted a job more. If I got the job, it would be my first time working alone as the enlisted aide to such a high ranking officer—the highest ranking black admiral in US military history. Reason wasn't yet the first black four-star admiral, but he had three stars.

I always carried a cross in my pocket and kept rubbing it with my fingers, saying, "God, please help me with the interview." Whenever I got nervous, I stumbled over words, and I needed to make a good impression. I told Admiral Reason about the time I saw him out in Seattle, when I said to myself that I would work for him some day.

"Really? That's neat."

He asked me about cooking, cleaning, and taking care of his uniform.

"If we leave things lying around, do you mind picking up after us?"

"Not at all, sir, because that's my job, to take care of you guys, to keep you happy. As long as the missus of the house is happy, then the admiral is happy. You don't want you to come home and find Ms. Reason complaining. When she's happy, you're happy."

"And so you're okay with doing my laundry?"

"Absolutely. I'm here to take care of you guys."

I was trying to be professional, but then a little of that southern stuff came out.

"Admiral, I cook gourmet food. The only thing I don't know how to make is soul food."

I was worried that I wouldn't get the job because I couldn't cook it.

Admiral Reason laughed. "Chief, we don't eat that no more."

I knew exactly what he was telling me—we'd both come much farther than that.

We hit it off perfectly, like two regular guys.

"Chief Sutton, I'm going to let you know my decision by the end of the day."

Twenty minutes later, I got a phone call from his staff, and in the summer of 1994, I showed up for duty at his home in the Washington Navy Yard.

I was tickled to death because it was an honor to work for him. At six feet five, he was an imposing figure, slightly taller than me. He and his wife had two kids. Their son was in the Navy. Their daughter, Becca, was around my age. Whenever she visited, the smell of her perfume lingered, the best perfume in the world. I'd say to Mrs. Reason, "Is Becca home?"

"No, but she was visiting this weekend."

I can still smell it to this day.

Admiral Reason was the deputy chief of naval operations, working right down the hall from the chief of naval operations. If you reached that position, you were guaranteed your fourth star.

The admiral was very friendly, spoke to everyone, and treated them all the same, from the enlisted ranks to the flag officers and VIPs. He was very down to earth while being extremely professional. He had grown up in DC, where his father was a librarian at Howard University, a professor of romance languages and director of libraries, and his mother, Bernice, was a high school teacher of biology.

Reason became interested in the Naval Reserve Officer Training Corps while in high school but was not selected although he ranked second out of three hundred applicants. Following this rejection, he spent his freshman year at Swarthmore College, his sophomore year at Lincoln University (Pennsylvania), and his junior year at Howard University. As he was completing his junior year at Howard, Congressman Charles Diggs Jr. of Michigan contacted him and encouraged him to apply to the United States Naval Academy. Accepted for the Naval Academy Class of 1965, Reason reported to Annapolis as a midshipman in June 1961 and graduated with a BS degree in naval science. He was commissioned as an ensign in June 1965.

In November 1996, after working for him for two years, Admiral Reason was selected for promotion to four-star admiral, the first African-American officer in the US Navy to reach that rank, and was assigned as commander-in-chief of the US Atlantic Fleet in Norfolk, Virginia. I attended his promotion ceremony at the Pentagon, with the admiral's wife and kids.

Then we packed up and moved into the Missouri House at the Norfolk Naval Base, located in a section of historic homes known as Admiral's Row. Steve Shott, my friend from Okinawa, came along to work as Admiral Reason's chef.

The Missouri House was a handsome, historic structure with a stunning view of one of the biggest naval bases in the world. A two-story portico with impressive columns faced Hampton Roads. Verandas extended from the portico on either side, and a side porch overlooked the water from the east. Mary Custis Lee, daughter of

General Robert E. Lee, had once held a luncheon in the building, and Governor Charles Evans Hughes of New York (later Chief Justice Hughes) was a guest at a breakfast party.

My sisters and brothers used to say to me, "Are you really in the Navy?" They felt I had a cushy job, not a military one.

And they were right—I had the best jobs in the Navy. A hard job that required multiple skills, but a great one.

Norfolk is where I first met President Clinton, at a reception hosted by Admiral Reason. I missed getting my photo taken with Clinton by a few feet when my friend snapped it at the wrong time. I was behind a rope line and shook Clinton's hand. There's a famous photo of a young Bill Clinton meeting John F. Kennedy, and that's the kind of photo I was hoping for.

To me, meeting him was almost like meeting JFK.

I was very proud to work for Admiral Reason, not only because he was a great officer but because he was a black man who had risen very high.

I felt I was part of history. When he walked out the door, I felt a sense of pride that his uniform was perfect and that his shoes were brilliantly shined. He looked good, and that was my responsibility. Admiral Reason's white shoes, which he wore in the summertime, were hard to keep clean, but there wasn't a single scuff mark on them when he left the house. The creases on his uniform were crisp, his medals were perfectly arranged. (By the way, the best way to shine shoes is with Kiwi Wax and pantyhose.)

When I was growing up, my dad was always on the road, and I didn't see him that much. When I joined the service, I saw him even less. Admiral Reason became my second father, my "Navy dad." He showed a deep interest in helping me grow professionally and as a person. He took me under his wing because he saw something in me and knew I had the potential to go a long way.

When we were on an overseas trip, he had a talk with me in the hallway of our hotel.

"Chief, you talk so fast that your words run together," he said. "It's hard for me to catch every word you're saying. I want you to teach yourself to slow down so people understand you. And always look a person in the eye when you talk with them."

At first, I was embarrassed by his advice. It was so out of the blue that it felt like a slap in the face from your aunt, but then I took it as a learning experience, something about myself that I could work on and improve.

I practiced slowing down the pace when I spoke, pronouncing each word individually instead of slurring them together. Shy since I was a kid, I'd always had a hard time looking people in the eye, but I made an effort to overcome that.

I had watched flag officers and general officers and sought to imitate the way they conducted themselves. But I had never met a black person who carried himself with such poise and sophistication, and I sought to emulate him.

Rumors were going around that Admiral Reason was going to become chief of naval operations, the first black man to hold that position. One day in the Missouri House, I asked him about it indirectly: "Admiral, are we going to be moving back to Washington?"

He said we weren't, then paused for a moment. He seemed a little down.

"Senior Chief, no matter where you are in life, there are always going to be people prejudiced at the top."

I didn't say anything in response and left the room. I felt badly for him. I said to myself: *This still goes on, and at that high level?*

I knew everything in the Navy was political. When I worked for General Herres, he wanted to promote me to senior chief, but when he asked one of his colonels, his military aide, for his opinion on that, the colonel told him I wasn't mature enough and didn't have good leadership skills. I was upset because I ran the show in the general's house, and one bad evaluation could ruin your chance for advancement in the military. It hurt me even more because the colonel was black, and I felt he was undermining me out of jealousy. Why would he do that to me, especially when there were so few of us working at the top? He didn't owe me anything because we were both black, but he did owe me fairness and respect. What he said delayed my promotion to senior chief.

In 1999, after thirty-five years of service, Admiral Reason retired from the military. We had a conversation.

"Senior Chief, what do you want to do after I retire?"

I had no idea. I was coming up on twenty years in the Navy.

"Admiral, I'm not sure."

"Do you want to be the valet to the president?"

The offer shocked me.

"Doing what?"

"The same things you do for me. You travel with him, wash his clothes, pick out his daily wear. When you travel with him, you cook his breakfast. You work seven days a week, nonstop."

It sounded like a great opportunity. The pinnacle of the profession I had chosen.

"How do I go about applying for the job?"

He said, "I'll take care of it for you."

CHAPTER FIVE

A Target from Day One

Although I had served the nation's top generals and admirals, I had no idea what it meant to be the president's valet. Working for flag officers was one thing; becoming the right hand assistant to one of the most powerful men in the world was entirely something else.

Admiral Reason had written a letter to the director of the military office at the White House.

> As Enlisted Aide, MSCS Sutton has assisted me on numerous official visits to nations in Europe, Asia, Africa, and Latin America. His performance has been uniformly spectacular. Keenly aware of protocol needs, he enjoys a personal reputation for reliability and integrity. He is a man of principle!
>
> I can commend MSCS Sutton to you as a top candidate for personal Presidential support.

A few days later, I received a letter saying that I'd been picked to work in the White House mess, which served the president, his senior staff, and foreign leaders. The two valets to the president were employees of the mess, so that's where I would be reporting before being assigned. It was July 1999, six and a half years into President Clinton's term and about six months after he was acquitted at his impeachment trial resulting from the Monica Lewinsky scandal.

I was excited and called Mom (we had a phone by now): "I'm going to work for the president."

"*Really!?*" She got right back on the phone, and the news travelled fast.

But there was a lot to go through before it became a reality.

I had to pass security clearances at the highest level. The presidential valet would have privileged information about motorcade routes, how Air Force One operates, and Secret Service protocols. He or she would have direct access to the president on a daily basis. Other than the First Family, no one is physically closer to the president than his valet.

I had three or four interviews with the Secret Service and mounds of paperwork to fill out. They dug through my childhood since the day I was born. They went over my school, family, and military backgrounds with a fine-toothed comb. They made phone calls, visited Kinston, and talked with teachers, friends, and family.

They especially made sure I wasn't coming to the White House to exploit my position politically or monetarily, by selling stories to the *National Enquirer*, auctioning off a baseball cap the president wore, or leaking information to the press.

I was a little nervous because there was a lot of paperwork to fill out. Everything looked good until I was asked, "What's this about an $80,000 Mercedes?"

"What? I don't have…"

"You've got a truck, an eighteen-wheeler that you bought."

Then I remembered: I had put my name on a truck loan for my brother Tyrone. I helped him make the payments, but I was falling behind. Then Tyrone stopped making his payments altogether. Two or three months later, he left the truck in Kinston and went to work for someone else without telling me a thing.

I was left with the vehicle and had to hire someone to drive it back to the dealer. I got a lawyer and settled the case out of court. Lucky for me, because it could have prevented me from getting to the White House mess.

After I finally passed my security clearances, I took some vacation time, knowing the job was going to be nonstop once I started. Finally, the letter arrived: *Welcome to the White House, report for duty.*

I was not initially assigned as a presidential valet; instead, I was working in the White House mess as head of the supply department. My office was in the old Executive Office Building. I was in charge of the White House food supply, from shopping to cooking, with five or six people working under me.

I was waiting for one of the valets who had worked for Clinton and several previous presidents to retire, which I figured would happen shortly, although no one knew exactly when.

When I walked in the White House, it wasn't the first time I was there. I had visited in the tenth grade, but I still had butterflies when I walked in the West Wing and passed the Oval Office.

My first day on the job, I met the sailors who were the staff of the mess, the small dining facility run by the US Navy located in the basement of the West Wing. The mess sat around fifty people at a dozen tables. The room featured wood paneling, nautical trim, and ship paintings. Table reservations were available to senior White House officials, including commissioned officers, Cabinet secretaries, and their guests.

There were several dozen Navy personnel working there, handpicked for this prestigious position, and they all knew that I was coming there to be the president's valet.

One of my first big assignments was working at the White House Correspondent's Dinner in August 1999. I arrived an hour or two before the president and made sure there was ice-cold diet coke in the room. President Clinton liked his soda *cold*, almost frozen. I'd keep his diet cokes on ice for hours before he arrived, and he'd let us know if it wasn't cold enough.

The first time I interacted with the president was at an event in Boston. We had the buffet set up for him, his senior staff, and a few other guests, enough for about ten people. The president, who didn't know me at all at that time, walked up and asked, "Hey, what's for lunch on the buffet?"

I froze. Couldn't say a thing, which had never happened before. I was used to being around admirals and generals, but not the president. His aide stepped in and answered for me.

The first time I served President Clinton was nearly a disaster. Two master chiefs were working in the Oval Office serving drinks and asked me to help them.

"Sam, President Clinton's going to take a diet coke."

"Okay."

I entered the room with a heavy tray, loaded with about fifteen drinks. Six or eight people were with the president—a foreign leader and Clinton's senior staff, seated in front of the fireplace.

When I bent down, President Clinton took the diet coke as I expected but also took a glass of water and a cup of hot tea, unbalancing the tray. *Whoa!* I didn't drop it but came pretty close.

There was an unreal quality about Clinton. His movements were slow and smooth, almost like he was a machine, not a person.

Before I became the valet and was still working in the White House mess, I accompanied the Clintons on a trip to Lake Placid, New York, where they stayed in a private home. Mrs. Clinton walked into the kitchen in the early afternoon and said, "Sam, we'd like to have dinner at five or six o'clock."

Immediately, I was a little nervous. I had two junior staff from the White House mess with me, but they didn't know how to cook. It was all on me.

I figured one of them could at least boil pasta, so I directed him to do that. Sure enough, he put the pasta in cold water and then boiled it.

Right then I said, *I'm in trouble now.* But I hustled and made the Clintons baked chicken, vegetables, and apple pie (I had never made one before).

Every time I saw Mrs. Clinton after that, she told me how much she enjoyed my pie.

I figured I made it through my first major hurdle.

After working for a couple of months, the lieutenant in charge of the White House mess walked into my office at the EOB and said to me, "Sam, you're not going to get that valet position."

I showed respect and didn't blow my top. "Sir, if that's the case, why did I come here then?"

"There are about thirty or forty eligible people ahead of you who want to become the valet to the president."

"But I didn't come here to work in logistics."

He made it clear that he was in charge and calling the shots.

End of conversation.

I was real hurt. No one gets anywhere near the White House without being a stellar performer, without being handpicked and recruited. I had outstanding credentials and excellent evaluations. I said to myself: *Didn't my recommendation from a four-star admiral mean anything? I went through all that security clearance for nothing?*

I found out that another senior chief had been gunning for the job. There were lots of other people wanting the job too. People the lieutenant favored. The valet to the president was a highly coveted position. Admiral Reason's letter had given me an edge over others who had been waiting in line, a letter that went over the lieutenant's head. Someone from outside his orbit, someone he didn't know and couldn't control, was upsetting the planned line of succession.

I didn't want to be the head of logistics in the White House mess (logistics, by the way, is a specialty in the military where minorities often end up). I didn't want a desk job. I wanted to be a hands-on worker like I'd always been. I was highly qualified to be the valet; had I not been, I never would have been recommended for the job by a four-star admiral.

So now it was a waiting game. The two current presidential valets had held that position for many years. Would one of them finally retire? Or try to hold on to the job forever, as many of them did?

While I waited, the two valets were bumping heads. They were always running to the lieutenant in the military office because they couldn't work together.

After about two months of conflict, they decided to transfer one of the valets to the White House mess and bring me on board. Three months after Admiral Reason's letter, in September 1999, I was promoted to valet, serving William Jefferson Clinton.

I didn't interview with the president but did speak with Gary Walters, the head usher for many years, who told me about the family and how to present myself to the Clintons.

"Sam, you'll be next to the president, his right-hand man. If the president needs anything, the usher's office will make it happen for you."

He gave me a tour of the private residence. I had already toured the area open to tourists, such as the Red Room, the Blue Room, and the State Room, but only people with special clearance could enter the private residence. My badge allowed me to go anywhere in the White House, unlike the staff of the mess.

We took the elevator to the second floor. On the east side were two bedrooms, with the master bedroom in the middle, the Presidential Seal on the wall.

Mrs. Clinton had a lot of fresh flowers around, and much of the decor was in colors she loved: green and orange.

I was a bit in awe standing in the president's bedroom. His closet had glass doors. It seemed huge to me, until I visited Buckingham Palace a few years later. But the president's bathroom had a seventies style and needed a renovation. When Mrs. Bush came in a couple of years later, she redid her bathroom and dressing room and installed floor-to-ceiling mirrors, the same style she had at the ranch in Texas.

I was most impressed with the Oval Office, bowling alley, and movie theater.

It was a huge operation. There were fifty to a hundred staff members in the residence, including three chefs, about five or six butlers, and two valets.

The valet who stayed on showed me the president's clothes, his cigars, and how to walk Buddy, the Clinton's chocolate lab.

I already had an idea what to do. It was the same routine, only this time for the commander-in-chief.

The senior valet and I got along.

"I'm gonna give 120percent," I told him, "and I'll never let anyone down."

The Monica Lewinsky affair had been over for months by the time I arrived, but I thought about it whenever I passed the president's sitting room and dining room that were right off the Oval Office.

I became more relaxed around Bill Clinton after I became his valet.

I arrived in the residence around 5:30 a.m. and waited for the president to get up. He was a night owl, working until 2:00 or 3:00 a.m. every night.

After a few days on the job, I got a call from one of his aides.

"Hey, Sam, is he up?"

"Not yet."

It was around 9:00 a.m.

"Sam, people are waiting on him. You need to go in there and see if you can wake him."

And so I did. When I walked into his bedroom, Buddy was right on the bed with him.

How do you wake the president of the United States?

Carefully.

Don't turn on the lights. Walk quietly to the edge of the bed. Use a small flashlight or your cellphone light to locate exactly where he is. Shake his shoulder gently.

"Mr. President…"

Usually that worked, but not always.

One time, I went back to his bedroom two or three times and couldn't get him up. He had a meeting at 9:00 and it was past 9:30.

"Mr. President," I said, shaking his shoulder, "the world's waiting on you."

That did the trick.

Although Clinton was a late riser, he made up for it by showering, shaving, and dressing in twenty minutes. Once, after playing golf in Florida, he had to go to a meeting and was out of his golf clothes and into his suit in half that time.

"Sam," he told me, "when you've been in politics as long as I have, you learn to dress quick."

He'd be gone in the Oval Office all day. Meanwhile, the other valet and I would wash his clothes, organize his suits, and shine his shoes, trying to get the routine down. The president didn't come over to the residence during the day unless he was having a lunch with the First Lady.

I put in long days, sunup to sundown, always adapting to whatever the president's schedule was that day. It was an all-consuming job, like being at sea. On duty for seven days, with a couple of days off now and then. If there was a crisis, the valets put in longer hours.

And as always, there was no room for error, as I had learned from working with admirals and generals for years. You and I can go out into public with scuffed shoes or a crooked tie, but not the president of the United States.

Clinton didn't return to the residence until maybe seven, eight o'clock at night. I'd help him with his jacket, turn on the TV, and get him a cocktail or a diet coke or a coffee. He ate dinner at ten, eleven o'clock at night. I'd be on standby until he went into his private area. When he closed the door, it was downtime for him.

Something odd happened one of the first times I travelled with the president.

I asked the other valet, "Are you going to ask the president what he wants to take on the trip?"

"Oh no, no, no," he said, "we don't have time for that. We just have to pack it."

Well, he packed about twenty pieces of luggage although we were only going to be gone for one or two days. To me, this was sloppy. He never took the time to communicate with the President or First Lady.

When we got to the destination and Mrs. Clinton saw all the garment bags, she asked me, "Why are there so many clothes?"

"Mrs. Clinton, I told him not to bring so much. The president doesn't need ten suits for a weekend trip."

But I was the junior valet, and the senior valet had been doing it this way for years. He was ready to retire and was not about to change.

The same thing happened on a visit to their house in Chappaqua. Or when the Clintons went to England with about twenty pieces of luggage to stay at Prime Minister Tony Blair's retreat.

"Sam, why did you bring so much stuff?"

I said, "Ma'am, the other guy told me to bring it."

They brought so many clothes to the Clinton's home in Chappaqua that they hid them in various closets throughout the house so Mrs. Clinton wouldn't see them. They had always done it that way without thinking. But I couldn't and didn't question the way they worked because I was the junior valet.

Yes, everything in the military was political. I had known that for a long time. Rising in the ranks meant finding the right connections, the right mentor who would take interest in you. People were always jockeying for positions and promotions.

But I wasn't prepared for how cutthroat working in the White House would be. Everyone was trying to get ahead of the next guy to be close to the president, whether it was to influence profound policy decisions or to get an autographed photo. There was intense competition, and I was caught up in it from day one.

From the moment I walked into the White House until the day I retired eleven years later, there was a target on my back.

People would step over you to get where they wanted to go. I learned that I had to watch my back. I knew from Admiral Reason that there was prejudice at the highest levels of the military and government. But it was far more than a black-and-white thing. I had a position a lot of people had been fighting for. Admiral Reason's letter had jumped me ahead of those guys. I learned pretty quickly that I had to keep a small group of colleagues around me, people I could trust. Even more than before, I felt I had to really prove myself. I had always felt that way, but now especially. Working in the personal quarters of the White House, I felt all eyes were on me, and I wasn't wrong about that.

Adding to the pressure was that the Clinton White House was a bit out of control. Interns were eating in the White House mess and walking in and out of the Oval Office during daytime working hours. When I travelled with the president, people were constantly going in and out of his hotel suite. Interns and junior military people hung out with him on Air Force One. When the president took off from the South Grounds in his helicopter, you'd see a lot of interns standing out there with family members.

It was out of control, too laid back, like no one was in charge. I wasn't used to it after years of following the military's strict regimen. I liked Clinton, but he seemed to let people do whatever they wanted.

And now, as the new valet, I was in the hot seat. Everyone was trying to use me to get to the president. Anyone I had contact with or who found out what I did wanted access—employees of the White House mess, chefs at the hotels where Clinton stayed, classmates and friends from way back when in Kinson, even complete strangers.

My family was no exception. They were very happy for me and looked up to me, but I wasn't stuck up. I was the same old Sam, no better than my siblings. They still called me Junior.

Yet I couldn't relax when I went back home to visit. I never talked about the White House, but they always brought it up. I even got annoyed at Mom. Everyone at our church knew I was a presidential valet. Complete strangers who found out what I did were now suddenly acting like my best friends.

"What's the president really like?"

"Sam, when can I get this photo signed by Clinton?"

"How do Bill and Hillary get along when no one's around?"

It got to the point that I'd leave the house if someone came to visit to avoid the attention and the questions that never stopped.

But back at the White House, there was nowhere I could escape. Employees of the mess, friends of friends, junior ranking staff—all of them had requests.

"Please do me a quick favor—have the president sign this baseball cap."

"My family would love to take a tour of Air Force One. Can you help us out?"

"Sam, how about getting us into the White House Halloween party this year?"

They wanted golf balls Clinton played with, pens he used, cufflinks he wore. They wanted to take a photo of the private quarters or a tour of the Lincoln bedroom. They would have grabbed his pillowcases and sheets had I offered them up. If the president used hotel towels during a trip, I made sure to take them to my room and mix them with my dirty towels before the housekeeper grabbed them.

But most of all, they wanted things signed—photos, baseball caps and jerseys, T-shirts, magazines with the president's photo, books, and basketballs. Souvenirs that many of them thought they could sell for big bucks.

It was all naked self-interest on their part, and some of them weren't exactly operating with a full deck. Many of the photos they wanted signed were counterfeit—photoshopped to show them standing with the president. And they weren't exactly quality counterfeits.

I'd listen to the requests but didn't pass them on.

Did I ever use my position to get things signed for myself?

Yes, but only occasionally.

On a trip to Japan with President Bush, I was served a special meal of Kobe beef that I hadn't requested. To show my gratitude, I asked the president to sign a menu for the chef.

Because I was a respected and trusted employee, the presidents would always sign things that I left for them. But I was always extremely respectful of this relationship and was careful not to misuse the privilege. When I left the White House, there was a stack of items sitting in my office still waiting to be signed that I refused to pass along.

People were constantly asking me if I could introduce them to Clinton. Most of these requests I ignored. But from time to time, I'd make sure that people who worked behind the scenes got a chance to meet him. At some events, I would tell a chef where to stand when the president walked through the kitchen to give a speech. If we were at a hotel, I'd let their staff serve the president and mingle with him, bring him water and pick up his plate. I wanted to give hardworking, unsung people a chance to be part of the excitement, and they got a thrill out of it. I did it to make their day, but I didn't abuse this privilege.

Women wanted to date me just to meet Clinton. Three or four of them led me on, then dumped me after they got their wish. Complete humiliation.

While it was understandable that civilians acted this way, I was surprised at how many military personnel, both senior and junior, butted heads with one another to try to get access. On overseas trips, senior military people fought to keep junior military people away from Clinton.

It also stunned me to hear retired generals and admirals talking badly about the president. He was our commander-in-chief, and military people were supposed to support him, no matter his policies or political party.

There were a number of times when I didn't like what Clinton or Bush or Obama were doing, but I kept it to myself. I was there to serve the president of the United States and to serve him 150 percent. I wasn't there to serve the people who were opposed to him or the First Lady.

It was inevitable that I became a target of envy because of my proximity to the president. I saw him when he got up in the morning, saw him when he came home at night. I was not his family, but as close to family as any outsider could be. I woke him in the morning, laid out his clothes, chatted with him as he got dressed, helped him put on his suit jacket. I cooked for the First Family when they were travelling, walked their dogs, and accommodated the smallest of their personal habits. I was the bridge between their private and public lives.

And for presidential valets, it had always been that way. According to the White House Historical Association, presidential valets have been "personal assistants, messengers, confidants, nurses, barbers, bartenders, waiters, public relations agents, and companions."

Some of the earliest valets, for Washington, Madison, and Tyler, were slaves. William Lee, Washington's valet, was the only slave freed in the president's will.

Many valets became unofficial members of the First Family. When President Abraham Lincoln's valet William Johnson, a freed slave, died in January 1864, the president arranged for a burial at Arlington National Cemetery and paid for the headstone.

Kosta Boris, President Hoover's valet, was described by *The New York Times* as "guardian of the children, handyman, factotum of the guests, an indispensable cog in the machinery of the household."

Irvin McDuffie, FDR's valet, helped him in and out of bed and to strap on the steel leg braces he wore. In addition to helping Roosevelt dress in the morning, McDuffie lifted the president into his wheelchair before delivering him to his office each day. George Thomas, JFK's valet, helped him into the brace that eased his painful back.

In working for Clinton, I performed the same kinds of duties that I had done for years in the military. What surprised me now was how much more power I had. My business card read: Valet to POTUS. The moment I showed it to a sales assistant when I was shopping for the president, they dropped everything they were doing to help me. They gave me gifts to pass on to him—cowboy boots, cigars, neckties. When Clinton left office, he had almost two hundred ties that people had given him as presents.

I could walk out of any store in the country with shirts, suits, gym clothes—anything I wanted—for the president to try on. The next day, I returned to pay for those items we were keeping, but if I were a crook I could have made a killing.

None of the presidents I worked for came into office with custom-made suits. Most of what they wore came right off the rack. And a lot of what they came in with wasn't in the greatest shape. Shoes with worn heels. Mismatched socks. The only president who came in with fancy clothes was Bush because he came from money.

Clinton arrived with only about twenty suits. Obama came in with about thirty, bought right off the shelf from Macy's and other high-end stores.

One day, I said to him, "Mr. President, you'd look really good in Brioni suits." But Obama wanted a union-made suit from the US,

71

not one from Italy. So we found a store in New York and ordered six for him. Nothing came from overseas.

The presidents received so many gifts of clothing that they often had one hundred suits by the time they left office. When the Clintons left, they filled the Family Room in the residence with items they wanted to give away, like a yard sale. The residence staff picked out what they wanted. Mrs. Clinton gave away a lot of her jewelry, dresses, and other clothing to the staff. For years, my mom proudly wore a couple of Hillary's dresses.

A large part of my job—and the most grueling part—was travelling with the president. There were endless details to take care of to prepare for the trips, and I often worked until two or three in the morning, starting all over again at 6:00 a.m. the next day. Organizing events is always a difficult process, but doing so when travelling through different time zones makes it even more challenging. There wasn't any time to recover from jet lag; sometimes we were lucky to get a thirty-minute cat nap. We had to jump off a plane and go right into a motorcade to a hotel or a speaking engagement or a summit meeting. The pressure was intense, and we had to be focused and on point. What shoes should the president wear? Are his pants pressed correctly? Is the coffee prepared? As always, there was no room for error.

Up to three hundred people would be in the president's entourage whenever he travelled overseas, including his staff, Secret Service, police, medical staff, and motorcade security. But with stateside travel, it was more like one hundred people.

If the president was going to New York City, we would arrive two days before and meet with the Secret Service senior staff in charge of getting the president from point A to point B. We walked every step of the route the president would take so everyone knew exactly which way he was going, whether it was for dinner, making a speech, or a photo op. After that three to four hour meeting, everybody got their badges, and everything was in place. I was the senior person for that site, make sure everything was all set.

Whenever the president arrived at a hotel, foreign or domestic, we set up a secure suite for him called the Hold. The rooms above and below the president's room had to be unoccupied, and the Secret Service set up shop across from the president's suite. Other suites were for medical personnel, the chief of staff, the press secretary, and national security. A whole ballroom at the hotel would be set aside for press and TV journalists.

The president's rooms would be blocked off two or three days before he arrived. Each person who had White House clearance wore a pin designating their assignment—Secret Service, medical, transportation, or mess.

During travel, we wore suits, not casual clothes. You couldn't dress flashy. Some of the guys had to be warned not to wear "pimp suits"—jackets with eighteen buttons, pointy shoes, and stuff like that. A lot of people in the White House transportation detail wanted to dress like southern guys, country boys. You couldn't wear a fancy suit to outshine the president.

Meanwhile, the request for personal favors, to be allowed in the president's presence, was nonstop.

Can you help bring my family to the rope line on the South Grounds?

Sam, I need Bill Clinton's assistance in getting my son out of the military.

Once when I was shaking hands with someone, he handed me papers to pass on to the president to get his son into West Point.

"The president has a lot on his plate," I said non-committedly.

Once he was out of sight, I ripped them up. Not from spite, but to protect the president's time—the papers were fake, not printed on West Point stationary.

Staff from the White House mess would help me carry the president's luggage—not their job—just to curry favor with me.

I had a close circle of coworkers I could trust. People who communicated with me and who consistently did a great job. People whose intentions I trusted. A handful of guys who had my back. Perhaps this rubbed some people the wrong way, but I needed them because I had a lot of people who were against me. That was true

73

in every job I had. Not only because of a black or white thing but because some black people were jealous and tried to bring me down.

Even senior military people were jealous of me. I blocked their access in a way that would not have been the case with a more accommodating valet.

I began to make enemies when I didn't grant their favors on demand.

I arrived at the White House residence at 5:00 a.m. and stayed until about 7:00 p.m., when the president returned from the Oval Office. I kept this schedule seven days a week. During the day, I washed his clothes, pressed shirts and suits, and reorganized his closets. I made sure he had enough clothes and personal supplies and did various other tasks. During downtime—and I didn't have much of it—I'd chat with the butlers who became my good friends, Buddy Carter and Ron Guy.

Details are crucially important when you're the valet. Clothes must be laid out correctly and every room has to meet the president's needs. When travelling, I would rearrange furniture to make him more comfortable. I learned each president's personal preferences. President Bush liked peanut butter and honey sandwiches and water at room temperature. He had a rigorous workout routine. President Clinton liked ice-cold soda, never worked out, and ate anything in front of him. He loved watching comedy shows during his downtime in hotels, almost like he had never watched TV before. Bush preferred sports.

When travelling, I made sure that any items the president needed immediately were packed on top. I always unpacked the First Family's clothes on white sheets to ensure that nothing went missing, because a lot of hotel suites were dark. My main responsibility was to make sure that the president was as comfortable as possible at all times. Sometimes that meant running a fresh shirt or tie over to the Oval Office in the middle of the day.

When the president was making a speech, I set out water on the podium to his right about fifteen minutes before he walked out on the stage. I placed a White House napkin on top so he knew it was secure.

Before I became the valet, I really didn't speak to the president when we were travelling. I stayed in the background. When he walked down hallways in hotels, the junior staff stayed behind closed doors until he went past. If he was speaking at a school or gym, I stood behind the stage listening. We always had a game plan with his hour-by-hour schedule, from the moment he got up in the morning until he turned in at night.

There was always the potential that someone in the kitchen could try to slip something into the president's food. The Secret Service did a thorough background check on everyone at the hotel, and we always had one of our mess guys in there with the chef to watch him cook the president's food, which was always cooked last, before Putin's or the Japanese Prime Minister's.

There were also small tricks to ensure the president's safety.

I'd walk in the room where the dinner was being held, see where the president was sitting, take his empty plate, and switch it with another leader's plate just in case it might be contaminated.

What our government would have done if the foreign leader got sick from the switched plate, I had no idea.

Meeting world leaders and celebrities was part of the job. During the Middle East Peace Summit at Camp David in July 2000, I was serving drinks to President Clinton and Yasser Arafat, Chairman of the Palestine Liberation Organization, who were meeting one-on-one in the president's cabin. My father always talked about Arafat when I was growing up, and there he was in front of me. His translator asked for coffee with sugar. When I was finished serving, out of the blue, I said, "President Arafat, my dad talked about you all the time when I was growing up. It's an honor to meet you."

After my words were translated, Arafat and Clinton both broke into laughter. I was supposed to keep my mouth shut but couldn't help it. Arafat stood up and shook my hand, as President Clinton smiled.

Clinton sent a personal note to me in August 2000, thanking me for my service at the Summit. It was an honor for me to receive the letter, but I just did my normal duties—filling water glasses, providing notepads, cleaning windows, emptying trash cans, making sure meals were served on time. All the simple but crucial behind-the-scenes details that make possible a major meeting between world leaders.

I often had brief but memorable exchanges with people I admired. I served drinks to Clinton and former President Nelson Mandela of South Africa in Tanzania in August 2000. I was able to tell Mandela how much I admired him.

At a Beverly Hills fundraiser, I met Baby Face, the singer. The menu was both high-end gourmet and down-home soul food—macaroni and cheese, fried chicken, black-eyed peas.

I also met Chaka Khan, En Vogue, Beyoncé, Jay-Z, Lionel Ritchie, and Evander Holyfield.

I found out that some people I admired had feet of clay. When I was in Tanzania during President Clinton's meeting with Nelson Mandela, Jesse Jackson's entourage was at the airport waiting for the president to arrive. I was in the advance detail and walked up to Jackson with hand extended to say hello. He brushed me off with a look that said: *why are you talking to me?*

But when Clinton arrived and I got the president something to drink, suddenly Jackson was my friend: "How are you doing, man?"

It was the same with Alberto Gonzales, Bush's Attorney General. He was friendly only after he found out I was the valet.

When I met Condoleezza Rice in the Oval Office, I introduced myself to her. I looked up to her as a black woman who had risen to the highest ranks in the government. I said a few words, but she looked right through me. But once she found out I was her boss's valet, she turned out to be great people, and we had a lot of good times together at Bush's ranch.

Clinton was smooth and charming, but I wouldn't call him laid back or relaxed. Bush and Obama made you feel at ease. Not Bill Clinton.

He was always on the go and never seemed to have any quiet time. He'd get up at nine or ten and kept on the go all day. He had people around him constantly. He'd eat dinner at 10:00 or 11:00

p.m. and be working until the wee hours. He loved to entertain and party. Obama spent time with the First Lady and the kids. He walked the dogs and hung out with friends. Bush got downtime by himself, exercising or riding his mountain bike.

Not 42. He was always on to the next thing, always on the run, and always late. When did he ever sleep?

On his motorcade route, Clinton would always jump out of his limousine and shake hands with people for five to ten minutes, especially if he saw kids waving flags. One reason he was always running behind schedule. He'd arrive at 10:30 p.m. for a 9:00 p.m. meeting because he'd been mingling with people.

But none of the presidents I worked for stopped in black neighborhoods, not even Obama. I'd see all those little black and Hispanic kids out there lining the street, but we would zoom right past.

I knew the president had to keep a tight schedule, heading to the rich neighborhoods to raise money, but why couldn't we stop once in a while?

Sometimes I'd say to myself, "Am I really doing this job? A poor kid from Kinston, North Carolina, working for the president of the United States?"

Despite the pressures and challenges, it was never routine for me to walk into the White House each morning. And I had learned a lot from my service with admirals and generals. Admiral Reason had taken me under his wing, one black person to another: "Keep your nose clean, Senior Chief. Always be aware of your appearance and the impression you're making."

I represented the admirals and generals in the way I dressed, conducted myself, and spoke. And in the way the admirals and generals looked when they went off to work in the morning. That was a reflection on me and my professionalism.

This had been my work ethic throughout the years, and it didn't change when I worked for Bill Clinton. Shined his shoes until they looked like glass. Got every last speck of lint off his suit. Made sure his jacket buttons were tight. If he was in a hotel with marble floors, I made sure to set down towels in places he might slip.

I paid attention to every last detail and never took shortcuts. When the president walked out in public or down the steps to a state dinner, he was part of me. When I saw the president on TV and his tie looked a little crooked, sometimes I'd call his staff and say, "You guys need to straighten his tie when you get the chance."

When family members or even people on the street told me, "Sam, you had the president looking good last night," it made me feel good. Real good. I was proud of what I did.

When President Bush flew to New Orleans to view the damage from Hurricane Katrina, his shoes got muddy. We rode in pickup trucks into the city. Furniture and household belongings were scattered about, and there was a terrible odor in the air. When we got back to Air Force One, I cleaned his shoes for him.

Some black people said I worked like a slave, that I was an Uncle Tom or a sellout who just cleaned up after white people.

People in my neighborhood back in North Carolina would say that or staff at the White House, people who didn't care for the particular president in office at the time.

Even family members would say to me: "Man, you're really into your job, you really take care of his shoes."

"Did you clean the president's shoes while you were down on your knees?"

"Do you wash his drawers? His socks?"

My response was simple: "That's my job, you know. And I do my job 150 percent."

My brother Beachey was in the military and loved Bush, but he once said to me, "You're an Uncle Tom taking care of a white person." He was half-joking but boy did it hurt.

"Stop staying that," I told him, "enough is enough."

I could have said to him: *You think I'm brown-nosing? Well, look where I'm at.*

I could have reminded him that when we raked leaves as kids, we went to the white neighborhoods because that's what Dad told us to do. Black families didn't hire black kids to rake leaves. They didn't have the money. So we knocked on the doors of the people who could pay us. Was that being an Uncle Tom? Or was it trying to make a little extra money to help the family?

Was I resentful that my mom had to work for white families? You bet. But I would have been just as resentful if she had to work for black families. It wasn't that she was treated badly but that she had to work so hard. And she did that kind of work until she was well into her sixties, gone for five or six hours a day. We'd be waiting to eat dinner with no sign of her, while my sister Pat was in charge of us.

And yet I never heard my mom complain. Not once.

Was she a sellout? Or just trying to feed eleven kids?

I could have said all that to Beachey, but it wasn't worth it. I love him, but I learned to keep quiet about my work at the White House whenever I was around him, which continues to this day.

I was taking care of the president of the US. I was there to represent him, to make him look good. He had to look perfect at all times. Bush would sweat like a racehorse, which showed up on the blue shirts he liked to wear. I always brought along an extra blue and white shirt for him, a fresh tie, and a backup suit, so he always looked good.

Obama was once getting on an elevator with a black tie, and I fixed it because it wasn't straight.

Mrs. Obama said to me, "Sam, you his mama."

I took care of the First Ladies also, when they travelled. They had assistants who worked for them in the residence, but I took on that role on the road. A lot of people have asked me, "How do you iron a gown?" Use a good iron with a lot of steam and work fast. Iron the tip of the gown quickly, and if it doesn't catch the gown you're okay.

I also took care of the clothes of the First Family's children, who were all girls during my time in the White House—Chelsea Clinton, Barbara and Jenna Bush, and Malia and Sasha Obama. Chelsea was sweet, but I didn't see her much in the residence. But when the Bush girls came in, I washed their clothes, fed them, packed their suitcases, and travelled with them. Same thing with Sasha and Malia.

My mom loved Clinton, loved Bush, and loved Obama. She once told me, "Son, it doesn't matter who the president is or what party he belongs to. I'm always proud of you and the work you do."

And that was good enough for me.

One time in Chappaqua, President Clinton and Mrs. Clinton were in the kitchen while I was making lunch. She had already announced that she was running for a senate seat in New York. As I stood there cooking, the president was walking around the kitchen, grooming her for what to say to the voters as she sat at the table listening, taking notes, and asking him questions. A conversation between husband and wife, like my mom and dad talking.

They would have made a good team if she had become president.

I accompanied the president to New York City in November 2000 for a "Get Out the Vote" rally for Al Gore. Luther Vandross was scheduled to sing that night.

As Clinton was getting dressed in the residence before he left for the city, he said to me, "Sam, what do you think I should talk about in New York tonight?" I was handing him his tie, helping him with his jacket, and the question caught me by surprise. I had to think for a second. I usually wasn't asked for advice on speechmaking.

"Mr. President, I'll be honest with you. When you have these town hall meetings, all the people are handpicked by your staff. You need to talk to people who are struggling, like a mother who's raising two kids alone because her husband left her. That's who you need to have asking the questions, the people who don't have anything. You don't see them in the crowd. People living in the rough neighborhoods and the projects are people who vote for you too. There's a mom out there who can't afford to feed her kids. That's the people you need to be talking to in the town hall, not the people who don't ask tough questions."

"Sam, you're right. You know, we don't have that and we need to have that. We need to hear from those people."

When he spoke in Harlem that night, I was standing behind the stage. After Vandross finished singing, the president made his remarks.

> This country works pretty well when everybody counts, everybody has a chance, and we all work together. And we get in a lot of trouble when we start trying to divide ourselves one

against the other—old or young, black, white, or Hispanic, straight or gay, people with disabilities and people without, rich or poor. You know, when we start dividing up the country, we don't do nearly as well as when we work together.

And the most important thing I didn't tell you before about this economic recovery is, it's the first one in 30 years that included everybody. We have the lowest African-American and Latino unemployment rate ever recorded, a 20-year low in poverty, the welfare rolls cut in half, child poverty down by 30%, average income up by $5,000 after inflation. We take everybody along for the ride. That's why we're Democrats.

He also made spontaneous off-the-cuff remarks that weren't recorded. He talked about helping the mother whose husband had left her, the mother who couldn't feed her kids. As I listened to him speak, I heard echoes of what I had said back at the White House.

The president had taken to heart what I told him.

Hillary Clinton was tough on people and very demanding. Everything had to be in order, and you couldn't be late. You had to be on her good side, and I was because I did exactly what she wanted and knew what frustrated her, like too much clothing in the closets or buying too much food. A huge buffet for just a few people annoyed her, a waste of money. I was careful not to move anything around the residence without asking, and I always let her know of any plans in advance. Guys before me didn't know how to communicate with the Clintons and did things behind their backs. You had to communicate with both of them to keep them happy.

But overall, the Clintons were easy to work with. When they were getting ready to leave office, Mrs. Clinton sat down with me in the residence and said, "Sam, I wish you were with us from the beginning, the day we came into office." That meant something to me. I was sad to see them leave because they were very good people.

A couple of days later, President Clinton made an overture to me on Air Force One.

"Sam, will you come work for us when we leave Washington?"

"Mr. President, to be honest, I would love to, but I'm not ready to leave the military." I didn't feel my finances were in order to be able to retire yet. It was too big a step for me.

I was also worried they might get divorced after the Monica Lewinsky business, and no way I wanted to get caught in the middle of that.

But what people didn't realize was that the Clintons were a partnership in every way—politically and personally. They were either going to survive together or go down together; there was no in-between. After the impeachment, they circled the wagons. The public didn't see them sitting on the couch in the residence holding hands, as I often did. A warm and natural relationship. There were no arguments and no drama, at least none that I saw or heard.

Whatever their imperfections might have been, to me they appeared to be the perfect couple.

To Sam — with thanks — Bill Clinton

With my mother Esther Sutton, my godchild Jalie Gonzalez, and
my sister Samantha, joining Pres. Clinton, Mrs. Clinton, and
Chelsea at the White House Staff Christmas Party, Dec. 2000.

Travelling with Presidents Clinton and G.W. Bush on
Air Force One to Pope John Paul II's funeral.

To Sam Sutton
With best wishes, + *[handwritten signature]* Bill Clinton

On Air Force One, April 2005.
(Photo: Eric Draper)

With Pres. Clinton with other White House valets, Jan. 2001.
(Photo: William Vasta)

To Sam — Luther looks good, and so are you! Thanks, Bill Clinton

In New York City with Pres. Clinton and Luther Vandross, Nov. 2000.

Golfing with the president in Martha's Vineyard, Nov. 2000.

On the rope line meeting Pres. Clinton in Norfolk, Va.,
1999, three months before going to the White House.

CHAPTER SIX

Eight Years with George W.

When George W. Bush came into office, he didn't want a valet. His father reportedly said to him, "Don't worry, you'll get used to it."

When Clinton left, it wasn't guaranteed I would remain on. Presidents often decided to bring in someone new, particularly if the current valets served a president from a different party. I kept my fingers crossed because I loved the job.

During the inauguration, there was word out that some of the previous valets were reaching out to Bush 41 to get the job serving Bush 43. I found out later that they met with Bush 41 at the White House after his son was sworn in. While those guys were downstairs trying to make a deal, I was upstairs putting away number 43's personal items and washing and ironing clothes. If I stayed on, I'd become the senior valet, not in name, because the other valet had more years of service, but because I knew the job better and did the job better. The other valet basically let me take over. He'd been slacking off for a long time, spending more time chatting in the White House mess than helping the president. Someone had to step up, and he was fine with it. We were on friendly terms, and I didn't put him down. He simply let me run the show.

If I stayed on, we weren't going to do it the old way. We weren't going to bring twenty suits on a weekend trip. I was going to keep the President and First Family happy.

At midnight on inauguration day, Bush 41 and Barbara Bush came upstairs. The former president introduced himself and said, "Will you take care of my son?"

"Yes, Mr. President." Right then I got the job. Apparently Bush 41 and Barbara Bush had convinced George W. that he needed my services.

Mrs. Bush gave me a big hug. "I hope you do a great job because he's not so easy to deal with," she said. "But I think you'll be okay with him."

I had been a little nervous at the beginning, but now I felt okay.

Soon after the new president arrived, shook my hand, and I told him my title.

"Will you be my personal valet?"

"Yes, Mr. President. I'm going to show you what we've got set up for you." I took his overcoat and hung it up for him. We did a little tour of his dressing room and bathroom.

"Everything looks good, Sam. I appreciate everything you've done." Bush told me he got up at five every morning and was ready to eat at five thirty.

I understood his father's comment about "you'll get used to it." Both Bushes were very independent people. Having people handle and rearrange your personal items can feel intrusive. We all like things done a certain way. We all like to do certain daily rituals by ourselves. I know I don't want anyone in my bathroom. I would find it hard to get used to a valet.

But I took that into account in the way I did my job. As with President Clinton, I set out to anticipate Bush's wishes. He had the highest pressured job in the world. My job was to make his life in the residence pressure-free. He didn't have much time to waste. I didn't want him to wake up wondering where his socks and shoes were, or what shirt to wear, or what tie went best with his suit. Set out what he needs, exactly where he wanted it to be. If he reached for something he needed, it was there.

I followed the news closely, particularly during moments of crisis, to anticipate what I needed to do the next day.

When he boarded Air Force One, Bush would immediately change clothes. He didn't want his outfit to be wrinkled during the flight. I would press his clothes during the flight so that they would be fresh when he landed.

I never said anything to him about the Clintons, and he never said a word to me about them. This was the protocol with every president I served. It was a whole new ballgame.

When Bush was elected, a lot of the military people didn't like him, which surprised me.

They said they preferred McCain or Gore to him. That was because Bush 41 was the gung ho type who went to war in Panama and Iraq, and a lot of military people were worried that his son would involve us in a reckless conflict. And it was the military guys who would be fighting that war, not the civilians.

When Bush 43 was elected, I heard the grumbling.

"*He'll take up where his daddy left off.*"

"*You watch, Bush is gonna clean up overseas.*"

And after the country was attacked: "*He'll use 9/11 as an excuse to go after Iraq.*"

A lot of military people didn't want to be in his presence, let alone serve him. And sure enough, a lot of guys from the White House mess got shipped out during the Iraq War. Instead of making peanut butter and honey sandwiches for the president, they were getting blown up by IEDs.

Like a lot of military people, when Bush ran, I was rooting for McCain because he was an ex-military guy. I figured he'd be a little more cautious than someone who had never served.

But I was happy that Bush defeated Al Gore because I had heard that Gore and his wife were extremely temperamental, sweet one moment and ready to turn on you the next. People said you had to be on pins and needles around them.

Not exactly the ideal work situation for a valet.

The atmosphere changed right away under George W. Bush. No longer were interns running around the White House without permission. He brought in a lot of the staff his father had. Great staff, mature people. The best of the best, hand-picked.

Unlike Clinton, he didn't tolerate any looseness. Be on time, don't keep me waiting. If the meeting was set for eight o'clock, you best be there at seven forty-five. Bush was always on time.

He read the Bible every morning at five a.m. and was at work by six. Unlike his predecessor, he was in bed by seven thirty, eight o'clock at night. He didn't drink and worked out every afternoon. He liked to ride his stationary bicycle, and we brought it with him everywhere he travelled. He was also an avid mountain biker, riding on trails for two hours at a time down at his ranch in Crawford, Texas.

He read his daily message traffic in bed every morning, often speaking to his chief of staff before he got up. He made a recording every night of what he did that day.

Bush had particular fashion tastes. His pinstripes, like those of President Bush Sr., had his name in tiny letters on the stripes.

He was concerned about not appearing out of touch in the way he dressed. He said to me, "Sam, when I do a State of the Union on TV, I do not want to wear a French cuff shirt because voters will think that I'm rich by looking at my cufflinks." He only wore them at black-tie events.

Trump wears cufflinks every day.

As with Clinton, the toughest part of the job was the traveling because of the pressure of coordinating all the many details. Making sure the Hold was all set. Making sure the president got his meals. Make sure the shaving kit and makeup bag were in the bathroom, the pajamas were set out, the bed turned down.

With Clinton, we took everything in the president's closet. When Bush came into office, I put a stop to that. I said to the other valet, right in front of the president, "The shoes he's wearing today, he can wear tomorrow too. He doesn't need three pairs. And he can wear the same black suit two days from now."

The president was in complete agreement.

I studied his travel schedule and, prior to each trip, showed the President and First Lady exactly what I was packing. There was no more sloppiness and lack of communication. The other valet stepped back and let me do 70 percent of the work. I didn't mind; the job was now being done professionally, not out of habit.

I knew how much space there was on Air Force One for the President's and First Lady's clothes. I would take what we needed for that trip, whether it was for a day or several days.

I'd say to Laura Bush, "This is what you're going to wear tonight, this is for tomorrow, and here's a change for when we get back on the plane."

"Oh, perfect."

"When I bring the coffee tomorrow morning, I'll bring in the clothes you'll wear. I'll walk in, knock on your door, give you thirty seconds, and then I'm going to put everything in the dressing room."

The details were highly specific and never ending. Everything had to be perfect.

Bush liked peanut butter and honey sandwiches. I made them at the last minute so they wouldn't get soggy or cold.

At the hotel, I'd take the snacks out of the fridge and replace the newspapers with the sports magazines Bush preferred. If there were flowers, I got rid of them. Too fancy. He didn't watch any news—no CNN, no Fox—but loved baseball. Bush was a simple guy.

One time, the other valet and I ate a bag of chips that were intended for the president.

When he walked into the room, Bush asked, "Is something missing?"

I fessed up.

"I don't want you guys to be eating anything because the taxpayers are paying for it. And that goes for me and the whole staff too. We're not here to have a good time; we're here for business. So take these snacks out of the suite."

He was no-nonsense in that way.

On September 11, 2001, I was at the White House waiting for President Bush to return from a trip to Florida. A TV was on, and I saw the second plane hit the twin towers. I stood there, not sure what I was seeing.

A Secret Service agent said to me, "Sam, you need to get out of here, we're under attack."

What?

When I got outside, I was walking between the White House and the EOB when I heard a thunderous explosion. A plane had struck the Pentagon. A minute later, I saw billowing smoke. People were running everywhere and sirens were howling in every direction.

I stayed outside because I didn't know what was going to happen next. In the late afternoon, I got the okay to return to the White House. Mrs. Bush and Vice President Cheney were in the secret bunkers under the White House.

My focus was always on serving the president, but now I felt a special urgency to do so.

When Bush walked in the White House that evening, he wore his commander-in-chief face: *don't talk to me, I'm going to war*. You couldn't say a word to him. None of the usual friendly banter. Hello Mr. P and that was it. He went straight to the Oval Office.

In the days that followed, I was getting to work an hour earlier, at 4:00 a.m. Bush would go right back to work after dinner. That schedule lasted for a month and a half after 9/11.

I was even more attentive to his needs. The intense pressure he was under was obvious. I made sure he exercised, that his Bible was on his night table, and that everything was just right.

I saw Bush cry more than a few times. When he went to Walter Reed Hospital to visit soldiers who had been injured and burned in the Iraq War, he was teary-eyed. One glance at him and I knew how heavy his burden was.

Right after 9/11, I attached an American flag pin that the Secret Service had given me to the president's suit lapel. He smiled when he saw it and kept moving. It became an icon during his administration. Every morning I made sure to pin it on.

I also kept crosses in my pocket for him. I gave him one when he walked out the door in the morning, and he handed it back to me when he returned. To this day, I've kept that cross.

As with President Clinton, I travelled extensively with President Bush.

Not too long after 9/11, we went to Afghanistan. We took helicopters from the airbase to the compound of the country's prime minister, flying right through the mountains. I knew I was in a war zone when Marines on one of the helicopters flying alongside us started shooting their guns. I thought we were under attack until I realized they were warning shots. This went on for twenty or thirty minutes: *don't mess with us.*

For security reasons, our helicopters touched down at different places at the prime minister's compound. I didn't know where the president's copter was, so I set out looking for him. There were a lot of snipers around. I followed the Secret Service and finally found the president.

The president's meal was cooked in big pots set on wood fires, while the cooks squatted on the ground. I made sure to sample his food before it was served and to swap his plate and glasses.

In 2006, we stayed at Tony Blair's private retreat, which was a lot like Camp David. The Blairs hosted a luncheon for President and Mrs. Bush at a restaurant outside London. Mrs. Blair had set the menu, which included broccoli. I told the White House mess that the president didn't care for the vegetable but not to change the menu—we didn't change foreign menus and the president would simply push it aside. But one of our staff told Mrs. Blair they were thinking of taking it off the menu, which upset her greatly. The vegetable stayed on the menu but probably not on the president's plate.

I then travelled with President Bush to Buckingham Palace, where we stayed two nights, and I was able to meet Queen Elizabeth II. Barry, her personal valet, told me where to stand during a black-tie event so that I wouldn't get in her path. President and Mrs. Bush taught me to bow when I met her and not to speak to her until she introduced herself to me. I was also told not to extend my hand to her and was mortified when I forgot and shook her hand.

Barry gave me two of their personal coffee cups as a gift. When Barry and his girlfriend came to visit the United States, I introduced them to President Bush in the Oval Office.

Presidents are often presented with gifts, especially when traveling overseas, but at the time I worked in the White House, they couldn't keep anything worth more than $250. At a summit in France, Italian President Silvio Berlusconi presented President Bush with a watch worth over $35,000. Bush took off his Timex, wore the gift watch during the dinner, and then gave it back.

Once when we landed in Omaha, Nebraska, they gifted President Bush with thirty cases of Omaha Steaks. What the heck were we going to do with that much beef? When we got back to Washington, we had steak night for the White House staff.

When Bush traveled to Saudi Arabia, the King gave him a cape made of lamb fur and leather, and a humidor with over one hundred cigars in it. Bush took a handful of the cigars and told me to return the rest to our ambassador to Saudi Arabia. The ambassador told me to keep them. The Secret Service tried to buy them off me— they were probably worth $150 each—but I just gave them away. I still have the pearl humidor. President Bush didn't smoke cigars but enjoyed chewing on them. He had nearly four hundred of them; some were Cuban, which he kept hidden.

The Saudi King also tried to give President Bush one of his horses, but even if it wasn't worth more than $250, there was no way to get it back to the US.

After our first visit to Saudi Arabia, I found a lot of items missing from Bush's room. White House staff members were taking gifts without permission. I put a stop to that, especially since there were six bottles of cologne in the room valued at three thousand dollars a bottle.

When Bush visited Russia, I had a hard time getting through security to wake him up at five thirty in the morning. Putin's security stopped me every ten feet to check who I was. Their English was as good as my Russian, but I finally made it through.

At one point, while we were staying at Putin's countryside retreat, I was asked by a military aide to take a message to Bush and Secretary of State Rice at Putin's compound. When I walked in and handed the message to Bush, Secretary Rice was playing the piano. Putin's residence looked just like an American-style house, not quite what I expected.

Putin came to visit Bush at the president's family retreat in Maine. During the visit, Bush Sr. drove his boat like a man possessed. My other memory is of walking past Putin's guesthouse in the morning to find him standing outside, bare-chested. We smiled and exchanged friendly waves.

President and Mrs. Bush were preparing for a foreign trip when their daughters Jenna and Barbara were making the news because of their wild teenage behavior.

The president said to me, "Sam, when Jenna walks out to the helicopter, I want you to block her with the garment bag so the press can't see her."

On the South Grounds, the press is always to the right, about twenty to thirty journalists and cameras. When we walked out, I positioned the big garment bag so that no one was able to photograph Jenna. Did the same when we got overseas.

Part of my job description—keep the girls out of the news.

The Bushes spent much of their summers at their sprawling ranch in Crawford, Texas.

Laura Bush was much more relaxed there than in the White House. One day, I caught her drinking right out of the kitchen faucet.

"Sam, before I became the First Lady, I did that all the time."

In the morning, she made her rounds in the house.

"Sam, what you want to listen to today?"

Her preferences were Motown, Mary J. Blige, Willie Nelson, country music, and rock. There was the First Lady, humming along, clicking her fingers, shaking her head. Always on the move.

She indulged in a single martini on Saturday nights and only while at the ranch. She was very reserved when traveling in her official capacity.

She loved to read and loved to clean. When I dusted her books, she was especially happy.

Working at the Bush ranch was hard because of the heat. I generally liked the first week, but after that, it was a struggle. The temperature routinely reached a hundred-plus. After doing all the household tasks and washing their dog Barney, I was too tired to sleep. But I kept it to myself and never complained. It was my job.

Barney, a Scottie, was my favorite of all the presidential pets. He had a lot of spunk. One time at the ranch, Barney got sprayed by a skunk and jumped in bed with President and Mrs. Bush.

He also chased and attacked the Secret Service dogs. I had to warn the agents to keep their dogs away whenever I walked him on the White House grounds.

When the president was travelling on Air Force One, I took Barney to Andrews Air Force Base, thirty or forty minutes ahead of time and let base security know when I was arriving. But one day, Barney spotted a K-9 and all hell broke loose. When I tried to pick him up, he bit me on my hand. I still have a little scar to this day.

The president wasn't happy. It was like one of his kids had been bitten. He picked up the dog in my presence and had a heart-to-heart conversation.

"Barney, let me show you what you did to Sam. Don't you *ever* do that again! You hear?"

Another time, Barney jumped on the back of a K-9, which tried to shake him off with no luck. One of the Secret Service agents fell down trying to control his dog while I struggled to keep Barney away.

That night, I told the President, who was in bed. He just smiled.

He liked it when Barney showed his toughness.

Jeb Bush and his wife visited the ranch a few times. She stayed in her room except to eat, while Jeb would spend time with the family. They were very low-key people.

Secretary Rice was also a frequent visitor. Now that she knew me, we were on friendly terms. She talked with me about her family.

But she could also be intimidating. I remember Bush once saying to her, "Man, you're some tough lady."

I almost got shot at the Crawford ranch. The Secret Service were waiting outside for the president to go to lunch. One of the agents was adjusting his holster and his weapon fired.

I didn't hear it in the house, which was soundproof. The bullet went through the window, which was special shatterproof glass. I had left the laundry room and was putting clothes in a closet when the bullet nearly hit me in the thigh, piercing the wall on the other side of the president's office. It was kept on the down low. No use worrying the public too much.

Mrs. Bush's cousin was an ambassador who was always calling the ranch to speak to the president. I was instructed by the president to "tell him I'm outside cutting trees." The ambassador called so often that he must have wondered if there were any trees left standing in Texas.

The president was constantly trying to get me to participate in his exercise routine.

"Sam, come bike riding with me."

"Mr. President, I'm scared of snakes."

"They only come out in a full moon."

"It's too hot, Mr. President."

It was a constant running joke between us.

"Sam, I'm going fishing on the pond. Why don't you come along?"

"Can't swim and afraid of snakes. You can have that, Mr. President."

During the G-8 Summit at Sea Island, Georgia, in June 2004, the running joke was that the president's residence was haunted. Maria, one of Bush's personal assistants, had left her shoes in the bedroom on the second floor and couldn't find them. Barney, who usually followed us everywhere, started acting up and wouldn't come up to the second floor. Maria never found her shoes.

Jenna got married on a hot afternoon at the ranch. A black preacher gave her away and then asked for money from the congregation. We held the wedding dinner under tents.

At one point, I went on a six-week diet where I ate hardly anything except for vitamins and shakes. I was cooking ribs one day and sampled a taste. The First Lady caught me.

"Hey, you're not supposed to do that!"

I hated the diet but lost a great deal of weight, almost fifty pounds.

My favorite cereal was Honey Bunches of Oats. At the ranch one day, I took out my new box and found it half eaten. When I bought another, the same thing happened. Turned out the president was eating my cereal every day. I had to hide it from him.

Crawford was a real small town. It seemed that no one lived there. One time, I was driving Bush's pickup truck and a cop pulled me over in front of a restaurant. When he got out of his old-style patrol car, I was a bit nervous. There weren't too many black folks in Crawford.

"License and registration, please."

"Yes, sir." I showed him my White House credentials. He ran my information through the system and then walked back. He was real friendly. He knew the president was in town.

"You didn't come to complete stop back there. I want you to be safe, okay? Make sure you stop the next time."

"Yes, sir," I said, trying not to laugh.

He looked exactly like Barney Fife from *Mayberry RFD*.

When President Bush was campaigning for his second term, I travelled with him on his bus to dozens of small towns. People would be waving at him, and he'd yell back, "I love your dog!" and "Get out and vote!" He was getting huge crowds. I'd serve him lunch on the bus and then we'd drive to the next town.

I started noticing the pressure of the office weighing on him in his third and fourth years, and during his second term, his schedule slowed down a bit. He spent more time at the ranch rather than going on vacations.

He started losing his hair, which concerned him greatly, and he used a product to prevent hair loss twice a day.

They were a great family, from Bush 41 down to the grandkids. They may have been conservative Republicans, but they weren't stuck up, and I never detected a hint of racism.

What stood out for me is when President Bush supported my promotion to master chief petty officer. The other presidential valet was up for this promotion at the same time; he had asked Bush for a recommendation letter that helped him get the promotion because there were a lot of candidates we were competing against.

Several months later at Camp David, I asked President Bush if he could write a letter for me. He was a little upset.

"Why didn't the other valet tell me you were up for master chief? You guys work as a team. I could have written a letter for both of you guys. I want you to come follow me."

We walked over to his office, where he wrote the recommendation letter and handed it to me. It turned out the promotion cycle was over for that year, but the president got on the phone to make sure I'd get promoted the following year.

He was a simple person, a down-to-earth regular guy who happened to hold a high position. He wanted to trust the people around him, and he really trusted me because I never went behind his back.

The Clintons weren't stuck up either, but there was so much controversy and scandal going on with them that they were never entirely relaxed or unguarded. The Clintons were a business. For years, Mrs. Clinton wanted to be president, and she still wants to be president. I knew that back when I worked for her.

Clinton was smooth and slick. Bush was more genuine. He was close to the military, to first responders, to people who put their lives on the line. He'd shoot the breeze with you. *Sam, how's your family doing? How's your mom? Tell her I said hello next time you go home.*

We were very close for eight years, and I was always there with him. The other valet I worked with wasn't the kind of person to step up to bat, to go out of his way. Whenever he didn't step up, I was the one who did. If there were tasks to be done, I took charge. He didn't want to go to the ranch, and at times, there was some tension between him and Bush.

President Bush once asked me to do something. I said I'd take care of it. I came back in about five minutes and told him it was already taken care of.

"Sam, whenever I ask you to do something, you pass it on to someone else." He meant it as a compliment.

I was a master chief. I could make things happen. In my position, I was able to pick up the phone and say, "Hey, guys, you need to do this." I had a whole team working for me.

A lot of staff in the White House didn't go the extra mile. It was an honor to work for the president, but some people took advantage of the position. They wanted the prestige of the valet position but not the work that went along with it.

I was proud to be there and gave 120 percent. For more than eleven years, I worked seven days a week for the Clintons, the Bushes, and the Obamas. Working for them was my life.

I took pride in all the work I did, from helping a blind man shop to serving the most powerful man in the world. I never cut corners. I learned the hard way as a kid to do things the right way. And that will always be in my blood.

It was a job of many mundane and routine tasks, punctuated by moments that were quite the opposite and that I will always remember.

One day in January 2002, I was walking back from the Oval Office when in the hallway I passed a black woman wearing a scarlet red pantsuit. I hadn't walked more than a few steps past her when I realized who it was.

That's Coretta Scott King!

She was in Washington for the first celebration of the holiday honoring her husband and to present President Bush with a portrait of him.

I turned back, introduced myself, and said it was an honor.

Although I tried, I couldn't say another word, and neither could she. She took my hands in hers, squeezing them, shaking them lightly, as if to say, "You're going to be okay."

During the Bush years, the gossip and backstabbing at the White House continued all day long. People would smile in your face and stab you in the back as soon as you turned around. I was on the receiving end much of the time because I was so close to the president. I always had to watch my back.

There were only a few coworkers I trusted. The others wouldn't do what I asked them to do, although I was their superior. Instead, they chose to report to the White House mess.

I began to see more and more instances of people not doing their jobs or trying to undermine me.

The positioning of vehicles for a presidential motorcade is crucial, particularly when disembarking from Air Force One. If you lose your spot, it's hard to get back in. I began to see people positioning vehicles in a way that made it hard for me to unload the president's personal items. During one rainstorm, the positioning caused some of Bush's clothes to get wet.

On a trip to Europe, I caught some of the staff watching X-rated videos in the president's hotel room. What if Bush had walked in?

On the road, there were problems in getting the right food to the president. He loved his peanut butter and honey sandwiches. When I asked for them at the White House mess, I always got them, but on foreign and domestic trips, they gave me carrots and chips instead. Might as well have given me raw broccoli. I simply threw it in the trash. I couldn't tell if they were clueless or trying to make me look bad.

Probably a little of both.

They kept doing little things to hassle me. Ordered extra food at the hotel. Put chips in his car. A big buffet in the Hold. Beer and booze in his hotel room.

Sometimes they wouldn't pack small things that the president needed and I had requested, such as particular movies or books, or even the president's reading glasses. I counted on the people I trusted to fill in these gaps for me.

This behavior didn't start with Bush.

Back when I was working for Clinton, the mess gave me warm soda rather than the ice-cold diet coke they knew the president insisted upon.

If they packed too many clothes—especially when I was new to the job—I would look bad and get the blame.

There was steady sniping going on all the time. Did it have a racial component to it? I didn't think so. By then, the staff of the White House mess and the residence was pretty racially mixed. It was good old-fashioned office politics, acted out by oversized egos competing for a highly desirable prize—access to the most powerful man in the world.

At one point during the Bush administration, the military office at the White House didn't want me to communicate directly with the president. They wanted me to go through the lieutenant who was the head of the White House mess. The same lieutenant who said back in 1999 that I would never become the valet. He told me I had to go through him to pick out what clothes to pack for the president on trips.

"Sir, I need to ask the president questions all the time, like what he wants to take on a trip. Why do I have to ask permission from someone who has no idea what's going on? I'm the valet—why can't I ask him directly?"

"This is the new protocol."

They wanted me to pass all information through the military office—the clothes the president would wear on a trip, the meals he'd be served, his schedule. They wanted me to fill out a spreadsheet, listing his underwear and socks.

I filled it out one time, then ripped it up the next. I kept all that information in my head and never had a problem.

"Sam, we're changing our procedures," they told me, "to help the next person in the position."

In truth, they wanted to control the valets and remove them from the decision-making process. They wanted to control what time I arrived in the morning. What suitcase President Bush used. The number of socks, T-shirts, and underwear he could bring on a foreign trip.

I'd been doing this work for over twenty years. I needed someone to tell me what to pack for the president? What luggage to bring?

That new policy was shot down real quick, and I continued doing my job the way I'd always done it.

I didn't play politics, unlike the other valet I worked with. He regularly communicated with and kissed up to the White House mess. I only went there at lunchtime. I was in and out and didn't mingle with the cliques and in crowds. If I spent time talking to them, I'd be unable to finish what I was doing upstairs. Whenever I walked into the mess, the staff there wanted to pick my brain.

"What are Jenna and Barbara up to now?"

"What's new with the First Lady?"

"How's the president feeling these days?"

They wanted to know everything going on in the residence, but I never revealed much and went back to work as soon as I could.

I didn't let the lieutenant in the military office control me. I wasn't the type of person who jumped when told to jump. I knew exactly what I was doing, and I didn't want to answer to anyone but the president, his personal assistant, or the First Lady. I never took advantage of my position. Unlike some valets, I didn't take photos of the private residence. Or sneak friends and family to the rope line on the South Lawn. I shielded Bush, like Clinton before him and Obama after, from frivolous requests for favors.

President Bush once said to me, "Sam, I'm always signing photos for the other valet. How many cousins and nephews does he have?"

"Mr. President, those photos are for his golf buddies."

He was a little annoyed: "I want you to stop this." I talked with the valet, who agreed to end the requests.

A few months later, President Bush told the valet to throw out his beat-up pair of running shoes.

"Yes, Mr. President."

Instead, the valet took them home, telling me he planned to sell them on eBay.

When Bush found out, he was furious.

"Sam, I gave him those sneakers to throw in the trash, not to sell. Would you please go get them back?"

The mission was accomplished, and the other valet behaved himself, a skill which he had all the time in the world to master, given his work ethic. Meanwhile, I'd go to bed at two or three o'clock in the morning, and two hours later I was ready to go again, and I did this for almost twelve years.

Yet like the presidents I served, I couldn't please everyone.

A lot of my relatives and friends didn't care for Bush. They wanted a Democrat in office. All I did was listen when family members and friends went off on the president.

"I'll be glad when that guy is out of office."

"They had it in for Iraq even before 9-11."

"Can't wait until we get another Democrat back in the White House."

My only response was to tell them I had a great job. And that's all I told them. I never revealed my personal opinions or what went on behind closed doors.

When Bush was nearing the end of his second term, the other valet transferred to a new duty station, and we needed to fill the position. We had a great number of people to choose from, and the person that I wanted to bring in was someone who had started at the White House mess with me back in 1999. In addition to being highly qualified with years of experience, Robert was Latino, and there had never been a presidential valet from that ethnic background.

"Keep your nose clean," I told him, "and I'll bring you upstairs with me." For the next two or three weeks, I worked alone in the residence. I was optimistic about bringing Robert on board because the lieutenant in the White House mess, who I had butted heads with in the past, had left. But I heard that someone on Bush's senior staff was lobbying for a different candidate.

One morning, the president was in the bathroom getting dressed. He asked me my opinion on who should have the position.

"Mr. President, I don't have time to babysit any junior people." That was the extent of our conversation, but he knew what I was telling him. The other candidate just didn't have the experience.

A few days later, when the first family was sitting in the residence, the president called me over.

"Sam, the White House mess is shooting for the other guy to be your backup valet."

"Mr. President, I want Robert."

Meanwhile, I kept pushing Robert to serve the President and First Lady when we were down in Crawford so he could interact with them more. I liked the guy, he was good people, and he did exactly what I wanted done. He didn't have a swelled head; he was there to serve. I knew the President and Mrs. Bush would love him.

One night when the First Family was sitting in the residence, President Bush said to Mrs. Bush, "Laura, what do you think of Robert?"

She said, "He's a great guy."

Mr. President picked up the phone and said, "We want Robert." Case closed. A day later, Robert was upstairs.

Did this create more ill will toward me? Indeed it did. The person in competition with Robert was a yes-man that the White House mess felt they could control. Their plan was crystal clear: get their guy in and force Sam to quit. But that didn't happen.

At least not yet.

Having fun with presidential pets Barney and Miss Beazley on Air Force One, headed for Crawford, Texas, Aug. 2007.
(Photo: Shealah Craighead)

At the White House Christmas Party in
Dec. 2002 with four of my brothers.

With my brother and Pres. and Mrs. G.W. Bush,
Ft. Hood, Texas, April 2003.
(Photo: Eric Draper)

With Pres. G.W. Bush and my mother,
on my promotion to Master Chief, April 2003.
(Photo: Eric Draper)

The president congratulates me on my promotion.
(Photo: Eric Draper)

My last reenlistment in the Navy, Nov. 2005,
joined by Adm. and Mrs. J.P. Reason.
(Photo: Eric Draper)

Surrounded by family on my promotion to
Master Chief Petty Officer, April 2003.
(Photo: Eric Draper)

With Barney and Miss Beazley on the South Lawn
of the White House, Jan. 2006.
(Photo: Paul Morse)

In the White House private residence with Rev. Billy Graham, Oct. 2007.
(Photo: Eric Draper)

Greeting King Abdullah of Saudi Arabia, 2008.

In Alaska with my friend Sam Pleasant of the White House transportation staff, Air Force One in the background, Feb. 2002.

With fellow presidential valet Robert Favela, Jan. 2009.

Pres. G.W. Bush, Russian Pres. Vladimir Putin, and White House mess staff, Kennebunkport, Maine, 2007.

CHAPTER SEVEN ━━━━━━

The First Black President

A lot of people called Bill Clinton the first black president. He loved black folks and black people loved him. My mom adored him. I brought her, my sister, and a couple of friends to the White House Christmas party in 1999. It was a beautiful party for the press, Secret Service, and residence staff. My mom fell in love with Clinton, with how handsome he looked. In the photo we took, she was holding him real tight.

But Barack Obama was the first black president, and it was my great honor to serve him.

I felt I was a part of history.

A few months before Obama's inauguration, President and Mrs. Bush asked if I would come work for them in Texas. I told them the salary I wanted, and they haggled with me in a joking way.

"Sam, the cost of living is a lot cheaper down there."

It was tough to turn them down because I really liked them, but it wasn't really a question of money. At the time, I was leaning toward retirement—that is, until Obama directly asked me to stay on, and I was happy to change my plans.

On the day of Obama's inauguration, President Bush sent me a handwritten note.

> Laura and I will miss you. You worked very hard to help us for eight years. You did so with a smile on your face. You are a very good man and a dear friend.

We had come a long way from him not wanting a valet.

There's a very fast turnaround on inauguration day. The departing president is fully packed the night before and the incoming president must be unpacked as quickly as possible. The transition has to be fast and seamless. I was up until six o'clock in the morning packing President Bush's luggage and clothes.

At around 10:00 or 11:00 a.m., the movers arrived with the new First Family's possessions. I worked throughout the day and into the evening unpacking things, washing clothes, shining shoes, and touching up the new president's ties and suits. On and off, I caught a glance of the inauguration and parade on TV. I always had tickets but never could go because of my duties.

Around 9:00 p.m., the Obamas' Chicago friends began arriving at the White House. I met the president's cousins and friends, and Mrs. Robinson, Mrs. Obama's mom. I also met Malia and Sasha, who were adorable but quite shy.

The family and friends were impressed with the residence and particularly with the president's dressing room, where everything was highly organized. His suits and shirts were lined up in color order.

Around midnight, President Obama came upstairs.

"Hey, Sam, good to see you again."

"Same here, Mr. President."

His friends said to him, "You've got to see your dressing room."

Obama was equally impressed with the way everything was laid out. His closets had glass doors so he could peek at his entire wardrobe.

Every outgoing president writes a letter to the incoming president and leaves it in the bathroom on inauguration day. Why there? It's the only place it wouldn't get lost with everything getting moved in and out. Bush gave me the letter for Obama, and I placed it on the countertop.

There's an elevator in the White House on the staff side that has been signed by all of the presidents' children, a tradition that began with Amy Carter. I watched as Malia and Sasha Obama continued the tradition.

After working all day long, I left the White House at midnight.

The new president said, "See you tomorrow, Sam, bright and early."

I soon fell into the routine of serving my third President and First Family. I was now the senior valet, working with a junior valet who I'll call Victor.

I didn't have a say in picking him. A colleague I worked with in the residence said to me, "Sam, you need to find someone you can trust, who's not out to get your position." Victor was black, and I thought it might be better to have someone of a different race on the job rather than two black men taking care of the first black president.

Other than that, I was fine with the choice. I knew he was a White House mess guy and a yes-man. I still had to watch my back, but I also knew they needed me on the job because there was a new president to take care of, and I had thirty years of experience under my belt.

Performing the duties of a valet is an underappreciated art. It's not something you can master in a month or two. You have to be aware of a person's tastes, moods, inclinations, daily rhythms, likes, and dislikes. It's not a haphazard job. It's not casual or shoot from the hip.

It requires that you learn someone's habits and preferences intimately, and that you become alert and proactive in accommodating those habits and preferences. A good valet is like a good waiter: not intrusive, but not absent either. A good waiter is always aware of what his tables need. After you've eaten for a while, you're asked about the food. Water glasses and bread baskets are quickly refilled. If something is spilled, the waiter responds immediately. If you need something, the waiter is there, having anticipated the need.

A good valet operates in the same way.

From working for flag officers in the Navy all the way up to the president of the United States, I studied the person I was working for, from the first thing they did in the morning to the last things they did at night. What is his routine when he wakes up? How does he get dressed? What clothes does he like? How does he do his hair?

When he steps out of the shower, what should be laid out for him and where?

I picked up President Obama's routines pretty quickly so I could stay a step ahead of him. I knew his every move. After he showered and dressed, he always went to the family room to sit in a wingback chair and put his shoes on. I made sure that his socks and shoes were sitting alongside his chair. When travelling with him, I made sure to have his bottled water, reading material, and books at bedside because he read a lot.

Obama worked out every morning before he went to work. Mrs. Obama came in about twenty minutes later, and they worked out together with a personal trainer for a good two hours. After the president got cleaned up and dressed, he had his cigarette in the greenhouse.

For breakfast, he loved his eggs and bacon, while Mrs. Obama preferred oatmeal. They had dinner together every night at six o'clock. Mrs. Robinson was a private person who took care of the girls and dropped them off at school while the President and First Lady were traveling. She loved casinos and would occasionally sneak out to Vegas to play the slots.

Mrs. Obama made sure that Malia and Sasha read at least an hour a day. They were great kids, very respectful.

In addition to working out, Obama played pool to unwind. Buddy Carter, the chief butler, showed me how to make his favorite martini, and the president liked to relax with one or two on Friday and Saturday nights.

About a month after Obama's inauguration, the president was walking back into the residence from the Oval Office, and I was escorting him to his bedroom to help with his jacket. When we walked into the private sitting room, we saw Mrs. Obama sitting on the couch with her head down, crying.

"Sam, can you excuse us for a moment?" The president closed the door to the sitting room.

I knew the pressure they were under, the burning glare of the spotlight. Normal lives and privacy were gone. President Bush and his wife came from a political family and were used to the limelight, but the White House was a vast change for the Obamas.

And it wasn't the usual spotlight, by far. They were the first black First Family, and the stress was enormous. I knew Obama had been treated in a racist manner, and I knew lots of black people who were outraged about that. It wasn't my role or prerogative to voice my personal opinions or to offer sympathies to the president of the United States. Yet I felt deep in my bones what they were going through.

After he was elected, whenever I was visiting my family down in North Carolina, I overheard white people saying, "We don't need him because he don't know what the hell he's doing." Mom would say, "My son works for the president." And some white person would respond, "We need a better president than *that*."

And not just down south. I heard the same comments from military officers when I was on the road with the president. These weren't civilians mouthing off. I'm talking about military officers who had sworn allegiance to the president of the United States.

Had I heard lots of negative remarks about Clinton and Bush from people who worked for them? Yes, indeed. A lot of White House people were grumbling when Bush beat Gore.

But the level of animosity toward the new president was of a different order. No one questioned where Clinton and Bush were born. No one claimed they were Muslims or said they hung out with terrorists or raised doubts about whether they had earned their college degrees.

Same old, same old: a black man has to work twice as hard to get half the credit a white person gets.

I overheard uniformed Secret Service officers, who were sworn to protect the president, saying, "I'm not going to serve him." Someone on the White House communications staff transferred out, saying, "I'm not going to work for this guy." The staff member was white.

Was it racism? Or was it politics?

None of the presidents ever confided in me about the problems they were having. If they brought the job home in any kind of way, they took it to the First Lady, not me.

But when I was with Obama, one afternoon in his dressing room, six months into his term, he opened up just a bit. I was helping him with his suit jacket at the end of the day.

"Sir, can I get you a martini?"

"Yes," he said. As if to say: *I could use one.* "I'm having a hard time with the Congress."

I knew right away he had a rough day, and I couldn't help saying something, although it wasn't much: "Mr. President, you can't please everyone because it's not reality. It's just part of the job."

He smiled and said, "Sam, you're right about that."

I felt for him. When people talked badly about the president, I felt they were talking badly about me.

The Obamas had a lot of loyal, longtime friends working for them, like his special assistant Reggie Love and senior advisor Valerie Jarrett, which created a very casual atmosphere among the staff. Not chaotic like the Clinton White House but less formal at times. Some of that informality I liked. I usually wore a business suit as valet, but President Obama said to me, "Sam, on weekends you can wear a polo shirt and khaki pants if you like."

Other aspects of the informality were inappropriate. Some of the senior and even junior staff called the President and First Lady by their first names, a lack of respect compared with other administrations I worked in.

It bothered me because I knew what it felt like. Some of the White House staff talked down to me. I was a master chief petty officer, but some guys didn't address me by my rank.

I didn't mind being called Sam by the President, the First Lady, and coworkers who were close to me. President Clinton asked me, "How should I address you?" I told him my first name was fine. Same thing with Bush and Obama. They asked me and didn't assume anything.

But being disrespected by military people, both junior and senior, was a different story. Another master chief was addressed by his rank whenever he walked into the White House mess, but

I was always "Hey, Sam" to them. Why wasn't my record of service respected?

Did I say anything to them? No. I learned to live with it.

One morning, Mrs. Obama was sitting at the dining room table having her lunch. I passed by, carrying some laundry.

"Good morning, Mrs. Obama."

"Good morning, Sam." She was eating her lunch quickly. "I have a busy schedule today. Have to be out of here in five minutes. We always have people telling us where we have to be and where we need to go. I've got to keep moving."

"This job is going to keep you guys busy."

"I just have to get used to it," she said, smiling.

"You will," I told her. "Mrs. Obama, can I say something?" I felt protective of her, like I was speaking to my sister. "Your personal staff is calling you Michelle. You've come a long way. You're a role model. You've earned your title as First Lady. I think you should speak to your staff about that."

"Sam, I've noticed that, and you're right." She said she would hold a staff meeting to address the issue and thanked me for bringing it up.

Within about two or three weeks, I noticed a difference in how she was addressed.

I could be guilty of the same informality because the Obamas were so down-to-earth. I was helping the president with his suit jacket around lunchtime in the hallway of the private residence when I realized that I was standing in front of him with my arms crossed. I kept saying to myself, *He's the commander-in-chief—why are your arms folded?*

And yet I couldn't release them and stand at attention. Why, I don't know. It felt real awkward, like I didn't have respect for him, treating him more like a friend than the president.

I never did it again.

But young kids couldn't help calling him Barack.

When I brought my sister Peggy, her granddaughter, and my friend Melvin and his three young sons to meet the president, the kids were saying, "We're going to meet Barack! We're going to meet Barack!"

"It's President Obama," I said to them outside his office, "or Mr. President."

"No, we're going to call him Barack!"

And that's what they called him, but the president didn't seem to mind.

Peggy told me she wasn't going to cry, but the moment she stepped into the Oval Office she broke her promise.

President Obama's routine was to smoke two to three Marlboros a day. In the morning, he would shower, get dressed, and head to the greenhouse on top of the White House. Leaving the Oval Office for a break during the day, he gave me a heads up by nodding and pointing upstairs.

He had told me in the greenhouse on the first day of his presidency, "Sam, I don't want to smoke too much. In fact, I'm trying to stop. You hold on to them and just give me one when I need it."

I would pass him a cigarette on the way to the greenhouse. When he left, he stopped in the staff bathroom to brush his teeth before heading to the Oval Office. Then, after dinner, I cleared a path for him to sneak out to the greenhouse again.

On weekends, he smoked a little more. He never smoked in front of people, and some of his staff weren't aware of the habit.

When he went on trips, I had to ensure that he had a room where he could stand outside to have a cigarette. When he golfed, he took a "bathroom break" after the fourth or fifth hole, and I passed him a cigarette. Then I cleaned up the bathroom.

It was my job to slip out under the radar to buy his Marlboros. A carton lasted him three weeks.

The First Lady was understandably concerned. A couple of years into his term, when he was about to turn fifty, she said to me, "Sam, I want you to help him quit."

She left it up to us to come up with a plan. The president and I decided that he'd get one cigarette in the morning, to smoke in the greenhouse.

Once in a while, he needed more than one.

"Sam, let me smoke half a cigarette." I'd hand him the one I carried around for those occasions. He'd take one or two puffs and that was it.

It took him a whole year, but he finally quit around Christmas 2011.

"I appreciate what you've done," the First Lady told me. "He doesn't smell anymore."

I often spent time with the First Family at their home on Chicago's south side. The first time I walked into that house, I told Mrs. Obama that it reminded me of the movie *Big Momma's House* with Martin Lawrence.

She said, "It really does."

I cleaned that whole house, all four floors, top to bottom. A lot of house to clean, and it took about six hours. Did the same with the Clinton house in Chappaqua and the Bush house in Crawford. I was a valet, cleaner, cook, and housekeeper—I did a little bit of everything. And dog walker, which I did eight to ten times daily with Bo, the Obamas' Portuguese water dog.

All the presidential pets slept in bed with their owners, except for Bo, who was too large to fit. He was a really sweet dog. Loved to take baths, and I could wash him with no problems.

There was a funny incident with Bo when we were staying in Chicago. President Obama was walking with the First Lady, Sasha, and Malia to a birthday party in the neighborhood, accompanied by the Secret Service in cars and on foot. The president was walking Bo, and I was carrying the birthday cake.

We passed a man cutting his grass. Obama greeted him with a hearty "good afternoon" and received a dirty look in return. *Who the hell are you?*

A moment later, Bo crapped on the man's lawn. Luckily, the homeowner had walked away and didn't see it. Neither had the First Lady and the two girls, who were half a block ahead.

"You got something?" the president asked.

"Yes."

A Secret Service agent handed me a sheet of paper towel and I took care of the problem.

Bo walked on proudly, pulling his owner along.

At times, I forgot Obama was president. He was so warm and self-effacing that I looked up to him like a big brother would, and sometimes he talked to me like one.

"Sam, how tall are you?"

"About six five, Mr. President."

"You know how to play basketball?"

"No, sir," I said, "never much cared for the game."

"If I was your coach back in Kinston, you'd be my center."

"But, Mr. President, I don't know how to play the game."

"All you have to do is stand there."

"Really?"

"Yeah, just stand there and jump for the ball. That's all I need you to do."

He was a great basketball player. In August 2010, the president celebrated his forty-ninth birthday by inviting a dream team of current and former basketball stars to play ball for wounded warriors, US troops who had been wounded in action. Reggie Love, Obama's personal aide who played college ball at Duke, set up the visit. LeBron James, Dwyane Wade, Carmelo Anthony, Derrick Rose, and Joakim Noah came, as well as retired legends Bill Russell and Magic Johnson. College player Maya Moore of the Connecticut Huskies women's team also played.

The game took place at a gym inside Washington's Fort McNair, a short drive from the White House. The event wasn't open to the public, but kids from a local high school got a chance to watch the president play and get autographs.

After the game, some of the players joined Obama and a group of his friends for a barbecue at the White House. A small tent and tables decorated with sunflowers and yellow and white tablecloths was set up on the grounds.

I travelled with the president to Las Vegas, where his suite at Caesar's Palace must have been about ten thousand square feet.

Obama loved to play poker. He'd play a little on Air Force One with Reggie Love and some of his junior staff, and before we left for a trip, he'd give me his debit card to get a couple of hundred dollars in small bills for his games.

In Las Vegas, he said to me, "Sam, can you pay for some chips?" The general manager gave me $200,000 worth. When I signed for them, I said to myself, *I could take these and cash them in.* That night, the president and his friends played poker until 1:00 a.m.

In general, Obama was a very light eater, but the night of that poker game, Tony Siack cooked him and Reggie Love big steaks with all the trimmings. They were so heavy that I dropped Reggie's. The president told me not to worry about it, but I'm not sure about Reggie.

As with all the presidents I worked for, we became close. We weren't personal friends, but I was more than an employee.

Passing through the private residence, I'd wish Mrs. Obama a "good afternoon."

"Good afternoon, Sam."

She loved TV, especially the show *House Hunter*, where you follow people's highs and lows as they try to buy a house. One of my favorite shows also.

"Which house do you think they're going to buy today?" she'd ask me as I paused to watch.

"I say number two."

"No, Sam, it's going to be three."

I looked up to her because she carried herself as a lady and as a proud sister. She was very attractive and looked stunning in gowns. She and the president deeply loved each other.

At Camp David in 2010, they had a birthday party for the girls. I spent the weekend there helping Mrs. Obama organize it, while the president stayed behind in Washington.

Sasha and Malia invited their friends from school in DC and their cousins from Chicago. We had set up a huge moon bounce, shaped like a castle. They and their friends were having a great time with it, and the girls wanted me to join them.

"Sam, come in!"

"No way." I'm a three hundred-pound guy. I had no business jumping around in a moon bounce.

They pulled me in, so what was I supposed to do? I fell down and got caught between the wall and the floor of the moon bounce, while kids were jumping all around me like crazy. I was all twisted up and couldn't move, let alone get to my feet. Finally, I managed to crawl out, helped by Sasha and Malia. They were pretty worried.

"You okay, Sam? I hope you're not hurt because you've got to take care of our daddy!"

When I was told that Oprah would be visiting Camp David, the news caught my attention.

By now, I had worked for three presidents, met a fair number of famous world leaders, and chatted with my share of sports stars and celebrities. There weren't too many people I still wanted to meet, but Oprah was surely one of them. She held a special place in my heart. I grew up listening to her. I had always looked up to her, a black woman who had come a long way.

When Oprah and her close friend Gayle King arrived, Mrs. Obama introduced me.

"Pleased to meet you, Sam."

She requested sweet tea, a southern thing—iced tea with a lot of sugar. My parents drank it all the time. Oprah said it was the best sweet tea she ever had. The First Lady, Oprah, and Gayle sat around gabbing like old friends. Later I spent some time with Gayle by the pool while Oprah talked in the living room with Mrs. Obama.

"Where you from, Sam?"

"It's a small town in North Carolina. You might miss it passing through."

It felt natural talking to another southerner. She noted that I hadn't lost my accent.

We talked about wanting to get back home to eat real barbecue. We chatted a while about her son, who was attending Duke. Oprah once said of her, "She is the friend everybody deserves," and I felt the same way after meeting her.

I travelled with the Obamas to Hawaii for their holiday vacation. I was the point man in charge of making sure the house was clean, meals were planned in advance and served in order, with the president always served last, and that all guests were taken care of. I got up at 4:00 a.m. to help the chef prepare breakfast and to ensure the Obamas had a special holiday.

One morning, Victor, the junior valet working with me, showed up late.

"You can't be doing this," I told him. "We have to be on time. If the president gets up early, we have to be ready to roll."

For the next two minutes, he cursed me like a sailor. What in the world? I didn't speak to him for at least half a day. Later he came by and apologized.

"You have to be on time from now on," I said. "I don't have the time to babysit anyone."

There had been previous tension between us. I had heard through the grapevine that he thought I was calling all the shots and not giving him any responsibility. Complaining about me to the White House mess.

I could have written up Victor for the way he spoke to me that morning, but I let it pass.

When we returned from Hawaii in January 2010, the First Lady wrote me a note.

Thank you so much for all your hard work during our family's stay in Hawaii. The President and I know how much effort goes into a visit like this, and we want you to know that we appreciate everything you did for us over the holidays.

With our family away from home and the ever-changing nature of the President's schedule, it was so comforting to know that all of us were in such good hands. Your flexibility and professionalism were truly impressive, and we are so grateful to have been surrounded by dedicated and skilled people like you.

We know it could not have been easy to be away from your family for the holidays, so please know that your sacrifice did not go unnoticed. Thank you again for your help, and thank you for the work you do every day. We simply cannot thank you enough.

With Pres. Obama and my friends Adrian, Kirsi, and Levi in Hawaii, Jan. 2010.
(Photo: Pete Souza)

Sam — Thanks for the great job you do every day!

In the Oval Office with family, April 2009.
(Photo: Pete Souza)

At Hampton University with family, May 2010.
(Photo: Pete Souza)

A personal note from First Lady Michelle Obama, Feb. 2009.
(Photo: Joyce Boghosian)

A note of appreciation from the president, Jan. 2009.

With Oprah Winfrey and Mrs. Obama at Camp David.

Chapter Eight

Betrayal and Triumph

I had accompanied President Bush to Israel during his last year in office. I went sightseeing in the streets of Jerusalem where Jesus had once walked, with a tour guide and Robert, the other valet. I saw a little kid wearing a baseball cap walking all alone toward me, jumping around with energy and excitement. When he was about ten feet away, he made a quick right turn and disappeared down an alley.

Who was that kid? He appeared out of nowhere and disappeared in a split second.

In my gut, I felt it was a message to me, a message from God that I should have a child in my life.

This feeling persisted when President Obama took office. I realized that I was getting to an age—forty-nine—when having my own family seemed increasingly less likely.

One day, I went to lunch with Ron Guy, one of the White House butlers. As we were waiting in line to order our food, I saw a white man talking to a Latino teenager. It was clear to me that the boy wasn't his biological son but that they had a very strong bond. As I watched them interact, something told me that he was talking to his adopted son.

I said to Ron, "It's time for me to try to adopt. I want to have a family before I reach fifty."

That same day, I went on a national adoption website. When I searched for kids ages nine to twelve, a handful of faces popped up. One of them was of a ten-year-old black kid with an exuberant smile and the same coffee-and-cream complexion as mine.

I said to myself, "That's my son."

The next day, I called the adoption agency listed on the website. I told them about the boy I had seen and asked if he was adopted as of yet. They called back about two or three hours later and said he wasn't. I began the process of being approved as an adoptive parent, a thorough background check not that much different from the one I went through to work at the White House—finances, work history, family history, etc.

I talked to Myra, a close friend in Virginia Beach, who had been a foster parent for years and had adopted several kids. What did I need to know and do?

Myra connected me with an adoption agency in Maryland. I met with them and showed them the photo of the child. I knew he would be my child someday and called him Sam, although that wasn't yet his name. I took classes at the agency twice a week for six weeks to learn how to deal with kids like him—older kids who had a history of emotional, physical, and substance abuse in their backgrounds, and who had spent many years in foster care.

I learned that Sam's parents were just nineteen when he was born. His mother was white and his father was black. He hardly knew his dad, who was affiliated with gangs and didn't live with them. Serious addiction ran through his mother's side of the family; she abandoned him when he was four.

Sam had been alternating between a foster family and group homes for years. At age six, he tried to commit suicide. He had problems using the bathroom and was still wearing pull-up diapers at age ten.

I learned from my classes that a lot of adoptions failed when kids with problems like Sam turned on their adoptive parents. There was a very strong chance that Sam and I would fail as well. One of the adoption counselors asked me: "Do you still want to do this?"

"Yes," I said, "God is putting us together."

I handed out photos of Sam in the White House mess. "That's my son," I told everyone. I was the happiest guy in the world although it was far from a done deal.

I had an interview with several adoption specialists while on a trip to Dallas with President Obama in September 2009. While he was making a speech in a high school, I was interviewed on the phone for forty-five minutes by three or four adoption caseworkers as I walked around the parking lot. I was very nervous and kept rubbing the cross in my pocket. I wasn't sure I said the right things but was told later that I did very well.

I felt God had brought Sam and me together, and I prayed every day that the adoption would go through.

Some friends and family weren't supportive of my efforts.

One of my cousins said, "You're going to have a lot of problems with a kid like that. Do you know what you're doing?"

A Navy friend I had known since Okinawa told me, "You're adopting a drug baby." I never spoke to him again.

What had happened to Sam wasn't his fault, and it was up to me to try to give him a normal, loving life. But some people didn't understand that.

I told the President and the First Lady about my plans and showed them a photo of Sam. They said he was cute and asked what I knew about him. They were extremely supportive of me. President Obama would ask me from time to time, "How's it going with the adoption?"

I travelled with the First Family to Asheville, North Carolina, in April 2010, where they were vacationing at a resort for three days. When I was serving the President and the First Lady, President Obama said to his senior advisor, Valerie Jarrett, "Sam's getting ready to adopt."

"I think that's wonderful," Valerie said to me. "But are you going to be able to do this while working in the White House? So much of your job involves travelling."

"Valerie is making a good point," Mrs. Obama said. "It really does take a village to raise a child. Sam, do you have family support?"

"Sure, I have people who can help me," I told her. In fact, I was making that up. My siblings lived a great distance away from DC, but I didn't want anyone to talk me out of it. I also didn't tell them that I was adopting Sam out of foster care, just as I had kept that fact from my family.

For the next ten minutes, as the president listened, the First Lady and Ms. Jarrett talked to me about the responsibilities of raising a child. They offered a lot of advice and encouragement, and at the end, Valerie gave me a big hug.

"You're going to be a great father, Sam—I'm absolutely certain of that!"

As I carried their plates and cups into the house, I repeated those words to myself. My home and finances were in order, but it was harder for a single man to adopt, and pretty soon, a child with a troubled history was going to show up on my doorstep.

Yes, you're going to be a great father.

President Obama was heading to Seattle in August 2010, right around Sam's tenth birthday. I wanted to use this trip to meet him for the first time, but I couldn't reach out to him directly because the adoption was still in progress. I called Sam's social workers and proposed that he and a few other kids from the group home get a tour of Air Force One. That way, the focus wouldn't be on Sam alone. He didn't know at that point that I was thinking of adopting him, and he assumed his agency set up the tour.

As we taxied down the runway after landing, President Obama and I were looking out the window trying to spot him. Nearing the terminal, we saw a group of kids standing with Sam's social worker.

"Which one is he?" the president asked. "The bigger kid?"

"No, there he is—the little short one with the khaki pants and blue shirt."

Obama said, "That's a real cute kid."

The president descended from the front steps of the plane as I followed. He greeted the state's governor, senator, and congressional representatives, who were standing to the right. Then he walked over to Sam and the kids, standing to the left.

"Hey, how are you kids doing?"

I was off to the side taking photos as Obama went down the line greeting them. Sam was last. Later, he told me that his heart was pounding. He was completely starstruck because he had never seen a president before.

"I've heard a lot about you," Obama said to him. "How's everything going?"

Nervously, Sam stuck up his hand to give Obama a fist bump.

While they chatted, Monica, one of the caseworkers, told me things were going well.

"You did a great job during the interview, and the paperwork is going through. By the end of the year, you should have him."

It felt so good to hear that. A police report had been completed in August. My dream seemed to be coming into place.

President Obama got into the Beast. He gave us a big smile and thumbs up.

I walked up and talked to all the kids. I didn't want Sam to feel singled out, but I did ask him a few questions.

"What's your favorite food?"

"Salmon with brown sugar."

"And your favorite color?"

"Black."

"How's school going for you?"

"Not so great."

Sam and the foster kids got their tour of Air Force One while I trailed behind with the adults. We walked through the entire plane, from the cockpit to the galleys. They sat in the pilot's seat. Saw the president's cabin and office. On the table was a birthday cake.

"Hey, isn't it your birthday?" I said to Sam.

"But my birthday was two weeks ago," he said.

"That's okay," I told him, "you can have another one."

He was quiet. I noticed his hands shaking under the table as the kids ate cake. The crew gave the kids gift bags. In Sam's was a presidential cigarette lighter, which I took back from him.

"Why can't I keep it?"

"We've got something else for you."

We packed up the leftover cake to take back to his group home and walked with the kids to the airport lobby, where I said my goodbyes.

I found out later a local television station interviewed him.

"How was Air Force One?"

Sam could hardly talk because he had never had a camera in his face.

"Better than first class."

In September, I returned to Seattle to have my first official meeting with Sam at his foster home. For years, he had been alternating between living in a foster home on weekends and in a group home during the week.

I drove to the address the agency had given me, not knowing what to expect. I hoped, even prayed, that it was a beautiful home. Turning down Sam's street, I leaned over the steering wheel, searching for the address. Then I saw the house.

Tall grass in the front yard. Uneven curtains hung in the windows. Outdoor furniture and broken chairs scattered about the yard. Weeds sprouted in the unpaved driveway.

There wasn't a white picket fence in sight. I was used to picture perfect in the Navy, where everything was spotless and in order.

"Is that the house?" I said aloud. I checked the address again.

No mistake. It was a decent neighborhood with older homes and one really rundown one—Sam's.

Fear overcame me. I drove around the block two or three times. Who was going to show up at the door? Were Sam's foster parents black or white? I didn't know. Down south, I didn't usually walk into a white person's house and was always on edge when I did because I didn't know what to expect. What would the welcome be like? Did the family have dogs?

The house didn't have a front porch. At least that way, I could shake hands before stepping right into a stranger's house.

I said a prayer to God. What was the right thing to do? My flight back to DC left at 2:00 p.m. I could still make it and call it a day. Perhaps I wasn't meant to go through with it.

But Sam was waiting for me. He had been told the day before that I was coming. I found out later that on the day of my arrival, he ate his breakfast, went right to the front window, and stood there waiting until I came—for five hours. Excited. Nervous. Happy that someone might adopt him.

But I didn't know this at the time.

Maybe I could just walk in, meet him and his foster family, and still not go through with it. Everyone would understand if I had second thoughts, if I couldn't handle the responsibility.

Everyone except for Sam.

I was perched right on the precipice. Stay or leave? Go forward or give up the dream? Whatever choice I made, it would be a huge turning point in my life. Perhaps the most consequential turning point of all. One I couldn't undo.

When I turned into Sam's block the fourth time, I parked in front of the house. His foster mother was peering out of the window expectantly. As I walked up the path, Sam peeked out alongside his foster mother, and I knew why I was there. To have a son to share my life with.

Sam opened the front door. He looked eager to see me. He later told me that the kids in the group home had told him, "One of the president's guys is going to adopt you." He said he was a little worried because foster kids don't exactly trust the government.

Gazing up at me in the doorway, he thought I was the biggest person he had ever seen.

"Hey, Sam. Good to see you again!"

I greeted his foster parents, who were white. Even though the ice was broken, I was still nervous. It was a small dark house even though the sun was out, and I couldn't get past how it looked from the outside.

"Come up to my room!" Sam said excitedly. "I want to show you my fish!"

His room had a small twin bed and a big fish tank. I crouched down and looked into it.

"What kind of fish have you got there?'

"Goldfish."

He held up a pair of Heelys sneakers.

"Check these out. They're brand-new! I've never had a pair before!"

They were quite torn up, obviously found on the street.

His foster mother stood in the bedroom doorway.

"Sam, you need to change your pull-up."

He changed them right there in front of me, not at all fazed or embarrassed. I noticed they were cheap pull-ups. The thought came to me immediately: *he doesn't have much, he loves what he has and takes care of it, but I'm going to do a lot better for him.*

We had dinner with his foster parents and their biological son. We got to know each other a little bit more. Sam told me he loved to fish and wanted to be a vet.

Back at his foster home that night, his foster parents told me more about Sam while he was in his room. He had tried to commit suicide in the foster home at age six, putting a rope around his neck, and after that incident, he alternated between the foster home and group home whenever his behavior deteriorated.

The next day, I picked up Sam to enjoy some time with him alone. We spent several hours in the Seattle Children's Museum. Although he was ten years old, he was small for his age and played with little kids who were much younger. After leaving the museum, we passed by a thrift store, and Sam asked if we could go inside.

I didn't want to. They reminded me of shopping with my mom, being handed worn shirts and pants with holes. But I did it for Sam.

He ran right to the sneakers.

"Look at these—they're real nice!"

They were as raggedy as the pair in his room. My heart broke once again.

"Can you get them for me?"

I talked him out of it.

"What size do you take? These look too big for you."

I couldn't buy him gifts, but I got the okay to take him for a haircut, which he badly needed.

On Sunday, his family cooked lunch for all of us—Sam's favorite, tuna casserole, something I never had before. That evening, I flew back to DC, at peace that I had made the right decision. And Sam thought so too. He told me later that he knew I was the right one.

In October 2010, President Obama made a second political trip to Seattle. We stayed in a downtown hotel with a view of the famous Space Needle. I had gotten permission from Sam's social worker and foster parents to bring him to meet the president before going to school.

The Secret Service brought him upstairs. He was wearing the same blue shirt he had on during our last visit—his only good one.

"C'mon, we're going to meet the president."

When we went in his suite, the president was in his room getting dressed. Sam took off his jacket. When the president came out, they gave each other fist bumps.

"Hey, Sam, how're you doing?"

I left Sam with the president as I had some packing to do in the other room. When I came back, they were at the window looking at the Space Needle.

Sam later told me this was a very important moment in his life, looking out over his home town with the president of the United States.

"What's this area called? What's Seattle like?"

Sam was explaining how much he loved the Pike Street Fish Market.

"Is it hard to be president?"

"Very hard, but you can do good for people. You have a lot of power, but you have to be humble to make the right decisions. A bad decision can stay with you for the rest of your life."

Obama was putting on his watch and fixing his tie.

"Mr. President, what's this?"

He showed Sam various knickknacks that people had given him and that he carried around in his pocket for good luck—military coins, clasps, a small cross, an American flag.

"Why do you have this cross?" Sam asked.

"That's to protect me," the president said.

The president gave Sam a farewell fist bump and left for his speaking engagement.

When I took Sam back to his foster parents, he asked them, "Do I have to go to school today?"

BORN TO SERVE

"You sure do," his foster mother said. "Unless the president of the United States wrote you an excuse."

By the fall of 2010, the adoption was going forward smoothly, but no date had been set. Sam and his foster father came to visit me in Washington for a weekend in October. While his foster father visited relatives in Virginia, Sam came to the White House, where I had clearance to take him all over. I introduced to everyone on staff who had been seeing his photo for months. I kept it in the White House mess so I could look at him every day.

I took him to the annual White House Halloween party. We went to the residence first, where he got a fist bump from the president and met Mrs. Obama, Sasha, and Malia. Sam was wearing an Indian costume.

I said to the president, "Sam's got some face paint on."

"No," Obama said, "that's war paint."

The First Lady asked him how old he was and where he went to school. He met Mrs. Robinson and talked with Malia, who was the same age.

The Halloween Party had an Alice in Wonderland theme. "The most intricate and coolest carnival you could ever go to," Sam told me later. Iron Man sets. The Royals from Alice in Wonderland. Photo booths. Dry ice punch. Live snakes and tarantulas.

Sam put a live snake around his neck to surprise me.

I'm sure you know how that went.

He came back to DC in November so I could take him to visit my family during Thanksgiving. We drove down to Kinston and stayed in a hotel. Sam was nervous the whole time at my mother's house. Once again, I saw his hands shaking. He was a little hard-headed and talked back a bit. He mostly played with the dog. I didn't tell my family about his bathroom problems because I didn't want to hear any negativity from anyone. At the hotel, I put plastic on Sam's bed to try to keep him dry.

A month later, I flew out to Seattle to see him. He was staying at his group home. I was allowed to spend some unsupervised time with him and took him to my hotel. I told him he could take a shower if he wanted.

"How do I do that?"

He was afraid to take one, so he sat on a chair in the shower.

On our way back to the group home, he went to the bathroom in his pants. I could see they were wet, but he said they got that way from leaning on my car, which was wet from rain.

At the group home, his pants got wetter and wetter. It didn't seem to bother him. He ran around playing with the other kids while I sat and talked with staff. I saw Sam's room: it had a twin bed in it with nothing else.

The group home had donated furniture. The kids had to ask permission to go to the kitchen or bathroom or even to go from room to room. Jail without the bars.

Pretty soon, I saw that Sam had made a bowel movement in his pants.

"Hey, Sam, I think we should change your pants."

"Why do we need to do that?"

It seemed like it was normal for him. I learned that he hadn't been to a therapist for two years because of funding problems.

I took Sam to lunch at a restaurant. He filled his mouth with as much food as he could before he began chewing. Then he ate it real fast and crammed his mouth with more.

"Sam, why do you eat like that? Why not put a little food in your mouth and chew it?"

"Because you have eat fast in the group home. They only give us a few minutes to eat."

They had thirty minutes to eat, and what they didn't finish in that time got thrown out. Sam said he basically had just two meals a day.

"If you want more food, I'll buy it for you."

He asked me for coffee too. A kid drinking coffee? It seemed like Sam wanted to grow up fast.

He stayed overnight with me at the hotel. I changed his pull-ups three times, but he still wet the sheets.

The next day, when we returned to the group home, I brought pumpkins back for the kids. The staff didn't want to deal with that and watched TV as I helped the kids carve them at the table. They ate TV dinners; no one cooked for them.

They played again after dinner. I'll never forget one little white kid with blond hair and blue eyes, about seven or eight, who wore cowboy boots. Except for Sam, no one talked to or played with him. I'd been told that he'd been in the system for years, never had visitors, and sometimes would scream for hours on end. He was sitting all by himself, so I went over. He apparently knew Sam would be adopted soon.

"Can you take me too?"

"Uhhh," I said, fumbling for the right words to say. But as we sat there side by side watching the kids at play, I didn't know what those words should be.

Back in Washington, after the visit, I was driving in my car at midnight one Sunday, returning home from spending time at a casino with Ron Guy, when I got a call. It immediately felt weird. No one ever called me that late. I heard the voice of someone who worked in the White House mess, a junior staff member—I'll call him Mike—who was an acquaintance, not a friend.

"Hey, Sam, how are you doing?"

"Pretty good," I said, wondering where this was going.

"Let's do lunch or dinner sometime. Are you coming into work tomorrow?"

I told Mike I was off on Monday.

"Then how about Tuesday?"

"Okay."

That ended the call. I was perplexed and confused. We had hardly ever talked at work. Why was he calling me past midnight to make plans? Why were we making plans at all? We had never hung out before. Why was Mike suddenly interested in having lunch?

I was still asking these questions when I went to sleep that night.

I woke up at around nine the next morning. The doorbell rang, and I noticed a black SUV parked at the curb. When I answered the door, three people in suits stood in the hallway, two men and a woman.

"Master Chief Sutton? We're from the Navy Criminal Investigation Office. You need to come with us."

"What's going on?"

"Master Chief, you need to come with us right now."

I finished dressing, put on my shoes, and followed them to their office at Bolling Air Force Base in southwest DC.

I was extremely nervous. I had no idea what was going on, but I knew it was something big. But how big and in what ways?

I was escorted to a small conference room where I faced two civilian investigators across the table, a black man and a white female. They introduced themselves and got right to the point.

"Master Chief, we're here today because you've been accused by White House coworkers of a number of serious charges—sexual harassment, sexual relations with junior staff, using alcohol and drugs, and selling drugs."

I couldn't move. I felt I was nailed to my chair.

"Are you serious? I never harassed anyone. I don't drink or smoke. I don't even throw parties."

They said that Mike and other White House staff members, as well as people from other commands—about eight people in all—had made accusations against me. The investigators revealed a few of their first names but not their last names.

I sat there thinking: *my thirty-year career is getting ready to end.* Sex with male and female staff? Wild parties in my home? Smoking and selling pot?

I didn't know what marijuana smelled like.

I couldn't even stand the smell of cigarettes. If a smoker came by my place, he or she had to smoke outside.

Sexual harassment? Sailors and troops always horsed around a little. Everyone did that from time to time to have a little fun, to put each other at ease, to keep up morale—a playful arm around someone's neck, a pat on the butt. But I had never harassed anyone, male or female. Ever.

Some people were out to get me, but why?

As they continued to outline the charges against me, I thought back over my career. How many real conflicts had I had during the years? Very few. There was the officer on the *Sampson* who was rude about the way I cooked his eggs. There was the chief petty officer in charge of the mess at NATO headquarters in London. We got in a big argument over something. I had never been spoken to like that before in the military. I told the admiral's staff member, "This chief just chewed me out for nothing."

Those were the only real conflicts I could think of.

But there was also Victor, the junior valet who had cursed me on the trip to Hawaii with the Obamas, when I called him out for being late one morning. When we got back to DC, he spread rumors about me in the White House mess. Friends I could trust would pull me aside.

"Sam, watch your back. Victor's telling stories about you. Saying that you don't do any work. That you leave everything for him to do. Just letting you know."

It was a complete lie, the exact opposite of what was going on. I took care of the more tricky assignments because he never took the lead. If someone didn't step in to do something that needed to be done, then I stepped in. I had always been that way. I was always a step ahead in taking care of problems. I couldn't let someone lead who didn't want to lead. I worked well with Robert under Bush because he pulled his weight, and we worked like a team. I trusted him to the point where I could take time off and be confident the job would be done.

Not so with Victor.

The investigators kept reading the charges against me. I didn't know what to say.

"Master Chief Sutton, while this matter is under investigation, you can't return to the White House or reach out to any of the staff there. That's for the safety of the First Family and for general security reasons. This no-contact order is effective immediately." In the meantime, I would be assigned to other duties. The investigation, they told me, would end by December 28.

My immediate thought was Sam. The adoption wasn't final yet. What if these accusations got back to the agency? The charges were insane, but what would be the price in fighting them? Sam had already suffered through three or four failed adoptions. I couldn't bear the thought of him going through that again.

Before I left, they took a mugshot of me, as I held the numbered sign in front of my chest. The investigator taking the photo said to me, "They're all lying. I've been in this job for a long time, and you can bet on that. Their stories don't match up. Chief, you have nothing to worry about."

If I had nothing to worry about, why was he taking my mug shot?

That night, I lay in bed, consumed by unsettling thoughts, the darkest moment of my life.

If I was partying, drinking, and drugging, how had I managed to last eleven years as a White House valet? It wasn't a position open to anyone who came along. You had to be rigorously vetted and only the best of the best made it through. I never would have gotten within ten miles of the White House had my record not been impeccable.

How was I able to keep up a backbreaking schedule of domestic and international travel with the president, often working twelve-hour days? Why was my top-level security clearance renewed in June 2010, when I was supposedly selling marijuana and sexually harassing my coworkers? Why did I receive glowing recommendations from Clinton, Bush, and Obama? Why hadn't the adoption agency, in their background checks, found any damning information about me?

I must have been a master chameleon to have served three First Families and received great praise from them, while living a wild and dangerous secret life.

As I lay there, the nagging mental chatter gradually died away. I knew who I was, where I came from, and all that I had accomplished. I didn't have to convince anyone of the truth because I had it on my side.

I slept well that night.

The next morning, it felt bizarre not to report to the White House, not to walk through the gates for the first time in over eleven years. It hurt me to my core not to be able to say anything to the President or First Lady. To disappear from their lives without a goodbye.

And without an explanation, although I'm sure the president got one when he asked, "Where's Sam?"

That morning, instead of reporting for work, I met with a female military lawyer at the Washington Navy Yard.

She reviewed the accusations, the file before her on the table. If the accusations were proven true, I faced demotion, a court-martial, even prison time. But she would do her best to try to save my thirty-year career.

She repeated what I had heard the day before. Most of the people making charges against me didn't witness any improper behavior on my part, but were passing along rumors that they had heard. The lawyer said it was all hearsay.

I felt relief, but it was only momentary.

"There's word going around," she said, "that the guy next to the president is in deep trouble. Now, you can fight these charges. We can go after your accusers. We can file counter charges against them. We can fight them tooth and nail. Or you can decide not to fight them and simply let the investigation run its course."

I'd have to prove they were lying, and that would be a nightmare. It would take months out of my life when I was in the midst of adopting a child. I couldn't bear the thought of the adoption falling through, of Sam never getting out of foster care. I didn't want to go through months of uncertainty, and I didn't want to bring anyone else down.

I decided I wanted to retire from the service after the investigation was closed, adopt Sam, and move on with my life.

The lawyer said it was likely I wouldn't face a court-martial but a smaller proceeding called an Admiral's Mast. Instead of a trial, a single admiral would judge my fate based on the results of the investigation. With no court-martial, there would be no screaming headlines: *Valet to Obama in Sex and Drugs Scandal.* As if the president, already savagely maligned by large parts of the country, needed that.

I let the adoption agency know I was going through an investigation. Because of it, I couldn't see Sam without supervision when I spent two days with him in Seattle in December. He was accompanied to my hotel by a social worker.

After spending a few days thinking about what the lawyer told me, I called the person I trusted most.

"Master Chief, how're you doing?" Admiral Reason said.

"Things are not going so well."

"What happened?"

I told him about the charges. I did most of the talking, and it was tough to get the words out. I felt quite nervous. He was the last person who I wanted to tell this story to, and there was a tear in my eye as I told him.

"Who's behind this?"

"The White House mess. I didn't do nothing, Admiral. Absolutely nothing."

"I believe you."

Now I really broke down in tears. It was so hard to give him this news.

"Master Chief, hold your head up high. You're going to be okay."

Then he advised me on how to conduct myself when I went before the Admiral's Mast.

"When you walk into the hearing, do so at attention and salute. Tell them Master Chief Sutton is reporting for duty. When asked a question, give short answers. Yes and no answers. Don't give long explanations. Remember, you'll be okay."

On a January morning in 2011, accompanied by my lawyer and a couple of close friends, I reported to the Admiral's Mast in full dress blues with my ribbons proudly displayed.

The admiral serving as judge had been sent the report of the investigation. The entire proceeding lasted less than five minutes. The admiral's expression told me that he felt the whole affair was bogus and a waste of his time.

"Master Chief Sutton, how do you plead to the charges against you?'

As he read them one by one, my response didn't vary.

"Not guilty."

"Not guilty."

"Not guilty."

I wanted to say more, to defend myself, but I kept it short.

"Master Chief, all charges have been dropped against you. This proceeding is now closed."

I rose to attention, saluted him, did an about-face, and left the room.

It was over and, by choice, so was my military career.

I had always been a professional. I did my job well, the way I was trained to do, the way I was obligated by my oath of service. I didn't play politics. I didn't mingle with White House mess. I wasn't the valet who would do anything for everyone. I tried to stay above the jealousy and backbiting.

But I had a target on my back since day one, and in the end, they finally got me.

I had been thinking of retirement when Obama asked me to stay on, and I happily changed those plans. Now it was really the right time for me to retire.

I had time to reflect on what had happened to me. About the politics of the White House mess. I had been nice to those guys. I often recommended people in the mess for domestic or international trips with the president. I didn't want to ruin their careers—far from it. I could have reported Victor for his behavior in Hawaii, but I did not.

And now this was the result.

It wasn't a black and white thing. Victor was black. It was a sad truth that some black people could be as undermining as some whites.

There were fiefdoms and cliques in the White House staff, as there are in any workplace, any organization. Presidential valets held a coveted position, and that created a lot of jealousy. Bush had put in a good word for me with Obama, and it rubbed some people the wrong way that I had stayed on.

I had worked so hard to get where I was, and now some bad actors had brought me down. Yes, they finally got me in the end and didn't suffer any ramifications as a result, but I also felt it was for the best. After being cleared of the charges, I had the option to stay in the military, but I decided to retire. I dearly wanted to keep my promise to President Obama, to serve him through two terms, but I walked away from the job to focus on building a new life with Sam.

I felt more and more that meeting Sam was fate. Had I not stayed on with President Obama, I may never have met my son.

When I informed the adoption agency that I had been cleared, I received final approval to adopt him. And that, in the end, made me the real victor.

Judge Eric Z. Lucas

TO: 8/26/11

Samuel Sutlon Jr.

Sir: Today is a mere
memorial to the great thing
that you have done.
Thank you!

TO: 8/26/11

Samuel DewAyne Sutton

It is my wish and
prayer that the joy of this
day goes on with you forever.

Sam meeting Pres. Obama in Seattle
before going off to school, Oct. 2010.
(Photo: Pete Souza)

CHAPTER NINE

Raising Sam

For the first time since I was a young kid back in Kinston, I didn't have a job. I reported to Bolling Air Force Base for a new assignment outside the White House while I waited for my retirement to go through but was told there was no assignment for me. So I was sent home in January 2011 to wait. My retirement would eventually be approved on October 1. I would leave the Navy after thirty-two years with an honorable discharge and my full rank.

But that was still months in the future, as I waited for Sam to arrive.

It felt disorienting to have no responsibilities, no work identity, no place to report to, to be paid to stay at home. Night after night, I had the same dream: I had been called back to the White House and was packing for a trip with President Obama. I was walking through the residence, trying to find the president to talk to him about his luggage, but I could never find him. Then I'd wake up.

It was three years before I stopped having that dream.

I felt I had let the Obamas down. Working for them one day, gone the next. I wanted to talk to them, to explain what had happened, to tell them I was sorry for how it ended. Buddy Carter told me, "Sam, the president really misses you." Part of me wanted Obama to get in touch with me, but I knew he had a country to run.

I called up some top White House aides, hoping to be considered for a civilian job after the retirement went through, but my calls were never returned. I heard through the grapevine, from friends in the White House mess, that some people were still talking trash behind my back.

Over time, I did hear from the White House. In 2012, I was invited to the unveiling of President Bush's official portrait. I was invited to Obama's Christmas, Halloween, and Easter parties during the remaining years of his terms.

I turned all of them down.

Why?

Partly because the invitations were always for me, not for me and Sam. I was hurt by that. The people sending the invitations knew I had a son. Usually presidential invitations stated that you could bring along a guest, but not my invitations. I didn't want to go if I couldn't bring Sam, and I felt embarrassed bringing him if he hadn't been invited.

But it was more than that. Going back to the White House would have given me an opportunity to talk to President Obama and the First Lady, but I knew how some of the staff would react—it would only cause more gossip behind my back. And I didn't want to be a phony. I didn't want to pretend I was happy to see the very staff members who had betrayed me. I especially didn't want Sam to be around that atmosphere.

But there was no bitterness on my part, none at all. I realized that God had opened another door for me, as he had done all my life. I was relaxed and at peace, because now I could devote all my time and attention to giving Sam a new life.

He came to live with me in January 2011.

I flew to Seattle to pick him up. When I walked into the courtroom, I saw Sam's sister, brother, and grandad standing with the social workers. The judge had no questions for me, only for Sam.

"Why do you want Sam to be your dad?"

"Because he buys me things and I love him."

"Where are you two going to live?"

"I'm moving to DC. Sam has me all lined up for school."

At that point he wasn't yet calling me dad.

The judge asked him a few more questions, then turned to me, smiling.

"Mr. Sutton, remember that you can't give him back." In his chambers, he gave us letters he had written, to both father and son.

When we got back to my house in Alexandria, I had his room all set up. When he walked in, I saw his hands shaking, a symptom of his PTSD. That night, he was scared to sleep in his room because of his intense fear of the dark, so he stayed in mine. After a week or two, he made his way to his bedroom and was able to sleep alone through the night.

If there was bad weather at night and thunder, I heard his footsteps heading my way. He was scared of loud noises. He had heard gunfire too many times as a young child.

He was still wetting his bed at night, and I kept changing the sheets and mattresses.

"You're going to be okay," I told him. "You don't worry about a thing."

After a month, he finally called me dad.

I hated seeing him go to school wearing pull-ups, but Sam didn't mind. "Go to the bathroom if you can," I told him, "but don't worry if you can't."

Two or three months later, he started wearing underwear over his pull-up, and he was so happy about that. But was still doing his business in them.

Throughout it all, Sam was a happy kid. He loved to bring home anything he found on the street—broken coffee tables, lamps, all kinds of stuff. He'd fill his room with that junk. It bothered me because it reminded me of going to thrift stores.

"Sam, why do you do that?"

"Because I was always sleeping in someone else's house as a kid, and I had to bring along my own things."

Once when I was cleaning his room, I found hamburgers and French fries hidden under his bed.

"Dad, I have it there just in case I get hungry."

"You know you can go in the fridge at any time, don't you?"

"Are you sure?"

"Yes, Sam," I told him. "You don't have to hide food. You're not living in the group home anymore. What's mine is yours. You can eat as much as you want."

Eventually, the food hoarding stopped.

He would arrive home with no homework: "The teacher didn't give us any."

A trip to the school solved that mystery.

"Mr. Sutton, all kids tell their parents that."

Sam was a very smart kid, but school bored him. Well, not all of school. He loved history and science, but he had a hard time with the social part of school. He got distracted by the drama and couldn't focus. He was small for his age until twelfth grade and got bullied a lot. Racial bullying. Sam was one of a small handful of black kids throughout his years in school. He had a high fashion sense even as a kid, which caused a lot of resentment.

And he was carrying a heap of anger, which he acted out verbally and sometimes physically.

It was real tough getting him to do his homework. But as long as he was doing well in school, I didn't argue with him about unimportant stuff, like cleaning his room. That could wait.

Sam's psychologist advised me on how to deal with his moods. He'd get very irritated if he couldn't find his keys. If he was upset, I didn't feed into it because that would only make it worse. If I saw his hands shaking, I knew it was best to walk away for a while and let him calm down.

He tried to run away twice in the sixth grade. When it got dark, he packed his bags and left. But he didn't close the garage door, which signaled to me that he planned on returning. He did it to distance himself from me because he was angry. He didn't want to say the wrong things.

I walked around the neighborhood calling his name.

"Sam! Sam, where are you? Why don't you come home? Sam!"

Because he was scared of the dark, I knew he wouldn't be out all night. I went home, left the front door open, and sure enough, he returned after about forty minutes. I left him alone, and after a while, he came down from his room and joined me for dinner.

I found out later he'd been hiding in the bushes down the block.

I didn't punish him or spank him when he ran away. I knew my father would have done that to me, but I didn't believe in it. I knew what Sam had gone through in life. I wanted him to be my friend, not my adversary. I wanted to help him through his problems, not make his problems worse.

Family members would say to me, "You spoil him. I was brought up being spanked."

But they weren't in my shoes. Nor were they in Sam's.

I'd say back to them: "Look at the connection we have. I must be doing something right."

Whenever I tried to get serious with Sam about his homework or cleaning his room, he'd say something that would make me put my hand over my mouth, trying not to laugh. He knew how to get to me. He was a sweet soul who wouldn't hurt anyone, and I could never do anything to hurt him.

Still, the challenges nearly overwhelmed me. During a particularly hard period, I called my sister Peggy.

"When it comes to his issues," I told her, "I'm lost. I don't know how I'm going to do this. It's too much to deal with."

"Do your best, Junior. It will get better."

At the time, he was doing nothing in school. I couldn't help him with his homework; the math problems baffled me. He was twelve years old and still couldn't use the bathroom. I was meeting with his teachers at least once a week. The schoolwork was too slow for him. He cursed out a teacher and was sent to the cool-off room. I tried to enroll him in a private school, but he didn't want to go. Although he had his three close friends over the house—Eddie, Oliver, and Dominique—he still liked to be by himself.

I thought I was at the end of my rope, failing as a single father. It was too much to handle. I prayed to God to tell me what to do.

One day, my sister Samantha called me. I had never asked a family member for help, but she must have heard back from Peggy.

"I'm coming to help you."

"You're married," I said. "You don't have the time for that."

"Junior, I have the time. We're going through a divorce."

Samantha lived with us for seven years, and it saved me and Sam. She cooked, she cleaned, she walked him every morning to and from the bus stop. She was his babysitter/nanny/mom.

I consulted with a doctor, who hooked up a monitor to his underwear. A beeper clipped to Sam's shirt would tell him when his underwear was wet. This helped him remember to go to the bathroom, and by age thirteen, he was finally through with pull-ups and accidents. We had gotten over a huge hurdle, and life was much better.

Until twelfth grade, when Sam fell in with the wrong crowd. He began taking pills and missed six months of his senior year. He was in and out of rehab, spaced out, not knowing who he was, and didn't graduate.

I was completely blindsided by his drug abuse. It was Samantha who said to me: *he's on something.*

Then I found pills on his floor.

In the throes of withdrawal, he got into a fistfight with my nephew Dylan. He was drunk, and I had to call the police on him.

He cut himself superficially on the tops of his arms, but whenever he thought of doing something more harmful to himself, he said thinking of me is what made him stop.

But then the great turning point arrived.

He stopped being mad at the world. Why? He told me that he realized everything was in the past. He didn't have friends because of his anger, but he didn't have to be angry anymore. He could just let it go to better himself. His anger about the past, he understood, was the root of his problems. Not the past itself, but how he held on to that past.

He had hit rock bottom with the drug abuse, and he could either descend deeper into it or pull himself out. He had been kicked out of school after having been given a second chance and was sent to an alternative school with very small classes. He knew this was truly his last chance.

Sam earned his diploma, not a GED. I insisted upon it.

And then in 2019, there was another great turning point.

He went to Seattle to see his biological mom. She was in a terrible place. She didn't ask him any questions but just sat there smoking with her boyfriend.

At that moment, Sam said to himself: *I'm not going to be like you. I'm going to change.*

And so he did.

He's now at peace with his foster care experience. He said if he had to go back, he wouldn't change it. That part of his past, he told me, has made him into the man he is today.

He's used an expression that I've often used throughout my life: some things happen for a reason.

And he's also told me: *"Dad, I'll be forever in debt to you."*

Sam, other youth in foster care, and foster care staff meeting
Pres. Obama in Seattle, Aug. 2010.
(Photo: Pete Souza)

Meeting Sam in Seattle and sharing one of
our favorite hobbies, Oct. 2010.

A Life of Faith and Service

In the twelfth grade, when I gave my life to Jesus Christ, Reverend Rainer told me that I was going to be a preacher. Because I was shy, I didn't believe that I would ever become one, but I was excited to know that God wanted me to preach his Word.

The same thing happened when my mom and I went to Bible studies together. The leader said, "Your son is going to be a preacher someday."

Even though I gave my life to Jesus Christ in the twelfth grade, I gave my soul to Christ long before that.

In the fourth grade, I slammed a door on my finger and said, "Goddamn it." I never cursed again. And I never drank or smoked. Which is why the accusations made against me were so stunning.

My life has been a life of faith. I believe that God sent Jesus to die for our sins. If God is for me, then who can be against me?

I know that I'm not perfect. I get up every morning and pray to God to make me a better person. I know I never would have come this far without his help.

I pray throughout the day for God to help me. If something gets in my way, I take a breath. *God, help me put this breakfast together real quick.* And then the angels come, and help is on the way.

If I saw the Obamas today, I might cry. Although it wasn't my fault what happened, I still feel I let them down. I really enjoyed working for them and never got a chance to say goodbye.

That's what I would want to say: "I really miss you guys, you were good to me, I'm sorry if I let you down, and I wish I could do it all over again."

That way, I could get some closure. Or perhaps I've gotten closure by writing this book.

They say, "No man is a hero to his valet," but Barack Obama will always be my hero.

I'm proud of my service to my country. I'm proud that I've been able to serve others.

I grew up with very little, worked in the tobacco fields, but always dreamed of a better life for me and my family. I've come farther than I could ever have imagined. Many doors have opened for me. I've worked for three presidents. I've met prominent world leaders and famous celebrities.

But the greatest act of this journey was adopting Sam, the fulfillment of raising him, and the joy of seeing him mature and grow and use his great talents to the fullest. He's now planning for a career in fashion design.

Mom is now eighty-three, barely getting around. Hip problems and diabetes. She still loves to shop and cook and has remarried to a preacher. I've kept the promise I made to myself when I was kid in Kinston: to take care of her so that she would never have to clean houses for someone else. I always sent her money, starting when I joined the Navy back in 1979. And I kept my promise that I would buy her a house someday.

If Dad was still living, he'd be eighty-seven. And I've kept my promise to him as well. "Junior, make something of yourself someday," he told me as a child. "Don't let anyone hold you back and say you can't do it."

I was born to serve. That service has afforded me opportunities that have richly blessed my life and my family. I've been around the world at least two or three times. I've been to all fifty states. I've sat in the president's box at the John F. Kennedy Center for the Performing Arts. When President Obama was awarded the Nobel Peace Prize in 2009, he handed me the gold medal he received when we got back to his hotel suite and said, "Sam, make sure to keep this safe."

That's a long way to come, given where I started.

When I joined the Navy, I wanted to be an architect. Next thing I knew, I was cooking and cleaning for admirals and generals. Sure enough, I fell into the same thing that my mother did. Yes, I've had that thought from time to time.

But like my son, I wouldn't have done it any other way.

I've received my share of praise over the years, for which I will always be grateful, but there's one letter that stands out above all the others—the one written by General John Shalikashvili, chairman of the Joint Chiefs of Staff, back in February 1994.

> Your tireless attention to detail, conscientious dedication to duty, and personal tact have been invaluable. Your professional performance in an incredibly difficult position, in which the responsibilities are heavy, the hours long, and the demands great, has been superb in every respect.
>
> I thank you for your selfless sacrifice and devotion to duty.

The pleasure was all mine.

ACKNOWLEDGMENTS ▬▬▬▬▬▬▬

I have many people to thank, not only for their help with this book, but for the love, loyalty, and support they have provided me throughout my life.

First and foremost, I acknowledge my heavenly father Jesus Christ, for he made everything possible.

My son, Sam, you have been the best addition and blessing from God unto my life. You have been what I needed to help me transition from service to service a little easier. All of our growth, challenges, and lessons learned together have been and will be used for the good of us. My love for you is a lifetime commitment, and I am forever grateful unto God for you.

Mom and Dad, you both are the instruments that helped set the example of my lifelong ability to serve others. You gave me the building blocks of life, and I am using them to serve. Mom, words can't express my true heartfelt gratefulness for you, but I want to say thank you for your continued lifelong love toward me and the love expressed toward Sam. Dad, though you are resting (may you rest in peace), I can't help but see you and the man you created in me when I look into the mirror. You both (Mom and Dad) are woven into the fabric of my life. Love you to life.

My brothers and sisters. Oh, what stories I could tell about each of you. My love for you is tailored to whom God has created in each of you. Thank you, family, for every prayer, every challenge, and every lesson learned. Each word, situation, and growth opportunity helped push me to where I am today, and today, I stand on the prayers of each of you to include Mom's, Dad's, nieces, nephews, and friends.

Thank you, Christopher D. Ervin, for your time and help with this book.

Admiral and Mrs. J. P. Reason (Admiral, you will always be my Navy dad). General and Mrs. Colin Powell, for being my heroes. President Clinton and First Lady Hillary Clinton, President Bush and First Lady Laura Bush, and President Barack Obama and First Lady Michelle Obama: thank you for the opportunity to serve. Bridgette Edwards and Sam Pleasant, my sister and brother from another mother, best friends for life. Robert Favela and Tony Siack, my White House buddies. Dr. Richard J. Tubb, Col. Cindy Wright, Tom Judy, and Tom Weichart from the White House medical team. William (Buddy) Carter, White House senior butler, who took me under his wing. Ron (Depot) Guy, my casino running buddy. Matthew Wendall, who makes the best fried chicken in the world. Wayne Cummings, Marco, Steve Shott, Frank Branch, and Angel. The team at the White House mess. Secretary of State Condoleezza Rice. Reggie Love, Don Brand, Blake Gottesman, and the one and only Sleepyeye, personal aides to the president. Valerie Jarrett, who supported me in adopting Sam. The White House military aides and the US Secret Service.

Al Desetta, thank you for taking on the *Born to Serve* project with professionalism and a continued guidance.

If I've neglected to mention you, please remember that you will always have a special place in my heart.

WILLIAM JEFFERSON CLINTON

January 10, 2002

President FY03 E8/E9 Selection Board
(Active)

To Whom It May Concern:

I am writing on behalf of <u>Samuel Sutton, Jr</u>
MSCS, USN, (SSN 232-13-7367) who is under
consideration for advancement to Master
Chief Petty Officer. Sam did an excellent
job for me while I was at the White House,
and I strongly recommend him for this
promotion. I believe he takes his work
seriously and serves this nation with great
honor.

Thank you for your time and attention.

Sincerely,

Bill Clinton

Pres. Bill Clinton recommending me for promotion
to Master Chief Petty Officer.

THE SECRETARY OF STATE
WASHINGTON

28 Feb 02

To: President of USN
Selection Board for
Master Chief

I have known Senior Chief
Samuel Sutton for over ten years
and have had the opportunity to
observe his performance over the years.

Sam is a solid professional
who is totally dedicated to his
trade. He is completely
reliable and a pleasure to be
with. I believe he has the
competence, experience and leadership
ability to be an outstanding Master
Chief.

Sincerely,

Sec. of State Colin Powell recommending me for promotion.

Jan 20, '09

THE WHITE HOUSE
WASHINGTON

Dear Sam,

Laura and I will miss you.
You worked very hard to help
us for eight years. You did
so with a smile on your face.
You are a very good man
and a dear friend.

I wish you all the best
in your future. We look
forward to hearing from
you.

God speed

George Bush

Pres. G.W. Bush, thanking me for a job well done.

ADMIRAL J. PAUL REASON, USN (Ret.)

16 April 2003

Dear Master,

You can only imagine the joy that Dianne and I felt when we received a phone call from Denise Stratton, CLF Protocol Office, telling us that your name was among that small handful of professional Sailors selected for promotion to E-9.

We both have felt for years that there was no MS in the Navy that exceeded your skill, intelligence, honesty, and patriotism. Now, a selection board has come to the same conclusion, and it's about time (smile).

Your accomplishments have been a source of pride for us, since we first met – years ago. We will continue to be proud supporters of our friend, Master Chief Mess Management Specialist Samuel Sutton, USN, for as long as we last. Congratulations!

Sincerely,

MSCM Samuel Sutton, USN
Military Office
The White House
Washington, DC 20500

Congratulatory letter from Adm. J.P. Reason.

Medals

- Defense Meritorious Service Medal (2)
- Meritorious Service Medal
- Joint Service Commendation Medal
- Navy and Marine Corps Commendation Medal
- Joint Service Achievement Medal
- Nay and Marine Corps Achievement Medal
- Navy Unit Commendation Award
- Navy "E" Ribbon
- Navy and Marine Corps Good Conduct Medal (5)
- National Defense Service Medal
- Humanitarian Service Medal
- Sea Service Deployment Ribbon (1)
- Presidential Service Badge
- Office of the Joint Chiefs of Staff Identification Badge
- Allied Forces Southern Europe Badge

ABOUT THE AUTHOR

Samuel Sutton Jr., Master Chief USN (Ret.).

Samuel Sutton Jr. grew up in Kinston, North Carolina, one of eleven children raised by a father who lived paycheck to paycheck as a long-haul trucker and a mother who cooked and cleaned and scrubbed for other families when she had more than enough work waiting back home. He lived in a house with no central heat and no hot water for baths or showers. His family didn't own a car, so they walked to church each Sunday—three and a half miles each way. To help his family, Sam picked tobacco for nine hot southern summers, from age ten until he joined the Navy at nineteen (and finally took the first hot shower of his life).

Joining the Navy in 1979, he embarked on a thirty-year military career, rising in the ranks to serve as an enlisted aide to the nation's top officers, including generals John Shalikashvili and Colin Powell, as well as Admiral J. Paul Reason, the nation's highest ranking black admiral. Then, in 1999, he became a presidential valet to President Bill Clinton and continued in that position for the next eleven years, serving presidents G. W. Bush and Barack Obama. He worked long hours in a difficult position that required tireless attention to detail, conscientious dedication to duty, and personal tact.

Now retired from the military and working in the private sector, Sam spends his free time watching movies, fishing with his son, Sam, listening to southern gospel music, and getting together with his large and loving family.

CPSIA information can be obtained
at www.ICGtesting.com
Printed in the USA
BVHW090011190521
607645BV00008B/1188